BUSINESS WORDS

Deirdre Howard-Williams
Cynthia Herd

Heinemann International
A division of Heinemann Publishers (Oxford) Ltd
Halley Court, Jordan Hill, Oxford OX2 8EJ

OXFORD LONDON EDINBURGH
MADRID ATHENS BOLOGNA PARIS
MELBOURNE SYDNEY AUCKLAND SINGAPORE TOKYO
IBADAN NAIROBI HARARE GABORONE
PORTSMOUTH (NH)

ISBN 0 435 28007 4

© Deirdre Howard-Williams and Cynthia Herd 1992

First published 1992

To all our colleagues and friends at the British Institute in Paris

Illustrations by
Alexander, Jane Hughes, Angela Lumley and Peter Thornborough

Typeset by Pentcor PLC
Printed and bound in Great Britain by
Thomson Litho Ltd., East Kilbride, Glasgow.

92 93 94 95 96 10 9 8 7 6 5 4 3 2 1

Contents

How To Use This Book

Notes For Learners and Teacher

To enhance vocabulary development and reinforce learning, *Business Words* moves from general to more specialized topics and vocabulary, and deals with complex subjects at different points in different contexts. You will benefit from this graded progression of units and recycling of material by working through the book systematically from beginning to end.

Flexibility is, however, a key feature of *Business Words*. Units are self-contained and can be used in any order. You may prefer to select first topics of particular personal interest or relevance. Either way, when you have finished the book, you can be confident that you will know 1,000 essential business words.

To get the most out of the book:

- Always read the instructions carefully and look at the example. Then write your answers on a piece of paper.

- Do not give up too quickly! Use the Word List (p. 80) to get an idea of the correct answer.

- When you have done all you can, use the Answers (p. 74) to check and correct your work.

- Keep the book handy for revision and reference.

Title: Before starting each unit, it is useful to spend some time thinking about the topic and any words and expressions associated with it that you already know.

Section A: Section A usually fills the first page and features graphics and simple matching, labelling or gap-filling activities. The aim here is to provide a foundation of basic vocabulary for the topic.

Section B: Short texts offer practice in reading business documents, reports and articles, and introduce further important vocabulary items. All these texts are closely based on authentic and topical business materials and particular attention is paid here to collocations and idiomatic expressions. The wide variety of vocabulary development tasks and activities featured in this section includes multiple choice, word formation, true and false questions, vocabulary networks, text completion etc.

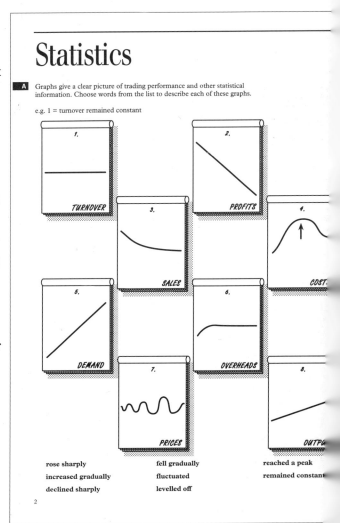

Statistics

A Graphs give a clear picture of trading performance and other statistical information. Choose words from the list to describe each of these graphs.

e.g. 1 = turnover remained constant

1. TURNOVER	2. PROFITS
3. SALES	4. COST...
5. DEMAND	6. OVERHEADS
7. PRICES	8. OUTP...

rose sharply   fell gradually   reached a peak
increased gradually   fluctuated   remained constant
declined sharply   levelled off

2

Section C: These short exercises may or may not be connected with the texts in Section B. They are designed to introduce additional topic-related vocabulary and, where appropriate, practise other skills.

Follow-Up Activities: It is best to work through these five questions in order. The first two items provide an opportunity for you to apply the vocabulary of the unit to your personal experience and professional situation. The last three items are designed to stimulate thought and discussion about wider business issues and possible future developments. Think about each question in turn and note down your ideas. Then try to find an English-speaker to have a good discussion, or use your notes to write a short report.

Before you start, read through these notes and suggestions for working through each unit. The first unit is used as an example.

TEACHERS:
If you work through the units in order, you will find plenty of variety to sustain interest and motivation. Alternatively, you can select units to fill specific lexical gaps and provide additional practice in a way that will complement other language course material in use, as well as your learners' professional activities or studies.

When you are starting a new unit, use the title to elicit any known vocabulary, to introduce the topic briefly, and/or to lead in to some preparatory discussion in class.

The activities in Sections A, B and C, can be done in class or for homework, individually, in pairs or in groups. With all exercises, it is a good idea to use homework time as advance preparation for the classroom as well as for follow-up assignments. It is also a good idea to have learners compare their answers and use the key to discuss them. This helps to identify any words which are causing particular problems and need more work.

How you exploit the Follow-Up Activities depends on the linguistic ability and professional background of your learners. An intermediate group should, with your help and support, be able to express some ideas on the topics and discuss them in class, pairs or small groups. A more advanced group could hold a class debate or round-table discussion. Encourage everyone to participate. As a starting point, ask individual learners to give short presentations, either to the class or to a small group (you will need to allow some preparation time for this, at home or in class). The subjects covered will lead on naturally to some form of written homework (for example a follow-up report, article or personal statement) which will help to consolidate what has been learned.

---

study this graph and read the article.

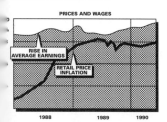

PRICES AND WAGES

RISE IN AVERAGE EARNINGS

RETAIL PRICE INFLATION

1988   1989   1990

Britain's inflation rate climbed to 8.1% last month, its highest since last summer and up from 7.5% in February. The underlying rate of inflation, excluding mortgage-interest payments, rose to 6.3%.

The main reason for the inflation increase was the March 1 rise in mortgage rates from 14.5% to 15.4%.

But there was a range of other price increases. Food prices, for example, rose 0.6% last month and have increased 8.7% over the past year. Seasonal food prices are 14.1% up on a year ago.

Official figures also showed that average earnings grew by 9.5% in the 12 months to February, up from 9.25% in the previous month.

omplete these three vocabulary networks, using the twelve words that are underlined in the text.

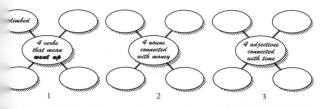

climbed

4 verbs that mean *went up*

4 nouns connected with money

4 adjectives connected with time

1   2   3

oose the word that is closest in meaning to these two words in text.

figures are: information/symbols/subjects/statistics?

earnings are: taxes/income/winnings/profit?

phs are one way of presenting data. What are these two other s called?

2

Follow-Up Activities

1 Choose a graph to explain – either from your own work or from the business press.

2 How are statistics presented in your company?

3 How can computers help to display data effectively? (graphics/screen displays/ spreadsheets)

4 Can we be sure that statistics are always accurate and up-to-date or can they sometimes present rather a false picture?

5 Statistics are becoming more and more important in the modern business world. Do we rely too heavily on them?

3

About This Book

What Is *Business Words?*

To succeed in today's increasingly international business environment, you must be able to communicate effectively in English, and that means knowing a lot of specialist terms and expressions. *Business Words* is a vocabulary development book that will help you learn the words you need.

Business Words consists of 36 self-contained units and features a wide variety of material and activities. It includes answers to all the exercises, and a word list with page references to 1,000 essential business terms.

Who Can Use This Book?

You need a minimum of lower-intermediate level English to start *Business Words*, but intermediate and advanced learners can also use it profitably.

You can use *Business Words* with a teacher - in class, in small groups or in one-to-one teaching situations. You can also use it if you are working alone: there are clear instructions and examples, with answers on p. 80.

Business Words is suitable both for students of business and for working professionals. The basic 1,000 business English vocabulary items it covers are needed by all learners.

What Is Special About *Business Words?*

Business Words is an interesting, varied and challenging book. It uses realistic and topical material to present vocabulary in context, and features a variety of stimulating tasks and activities for practice. There are also opportunities for oral and written work.

Business Words is designed to teach 1,000 basic words and expressions used in the world of international business. It also aims to build confidence in using the language and to expand vocabulary of a more general nature.

Each of the 36 units covers a different topic and is self-contained. The natural overlap between topics (for example, advertising, retailing, and marketing) has been used to promote learning by recycling vocabulary, concepts and contexts.

Business Words offers you the freedom to structure your own learning programme to suit your particular needs and abilities. It also encourages you to personalize the language you learn by applying it to your own situation.

Business Words is based on extensive documentary research and authentic material gathered from a wide variety of sources. This includes companies, trade organizations, and government departments; specialist press; and specialized reference works. It also draws on the authors' personal experience of teaching business English in university and business institutions.

Initial Contact

Statistics

Graphs give a clear picture of trading performance and other statistical information. Choose words from the list at the bottom of the page to describe each of these graphs.

e.g. 1 = turnover remained constant

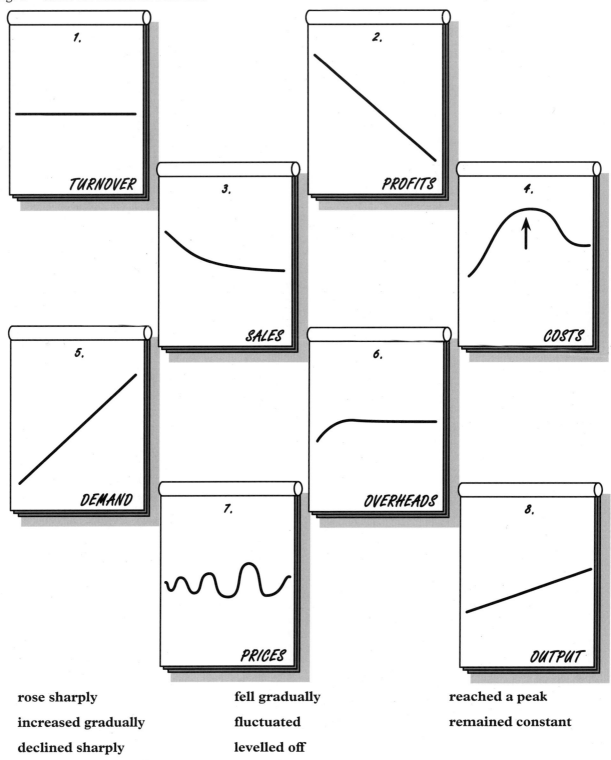

rose sharply

increased gradually

declined sharply

fell gradually

fluctuated

levelled off

reached a peak

remained constant

B Study this graph and read the article.

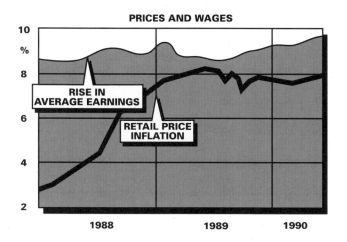

PRICES AND WAGES

RISE IN AVERAGE EARNINGS

RETAIL PRICE INFLATION

1988   1989   1990

Britain's inflation rate climbed to 8.1% last month, its highest since last summer and up from 7.5% in February. The underlying rate of inflation, excluding mortgage-interest payments, rose to 6.3%.

The main reason for the inflation increase was the March 1 rise in mortgage rates from 14.5% to 15.4%.

But there was a range of other price increases. Food prices, for example, rose 0.6% last month and have increased 8.7% over the past year. Seasonal food prices are 14.1% up on a year ago.

Official figures also showed that average earnings grew by 9.5% in the 12 months to February, up from 9.25% in the previous month.

Complete these three vocabulary networks, using the twelve words that are underlined in the text. e.g.

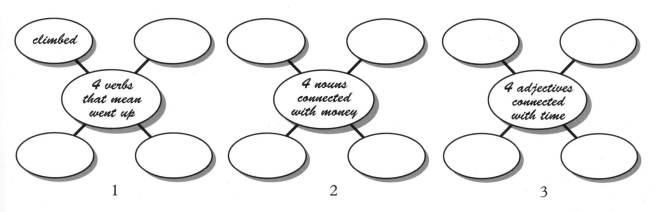

climbed

4 verbs that mean went up

4 nouns connected with money

4 adjectives connected with time

1   2   3

Choose the word that is closest in meaning to these two words in the text.

4   **figures** are: information/symbols/subjects/statistics?

5   **earnings** are: taxes/income/winnings/profit?

Graphs are one way of presenting data. What are these two other ways called?

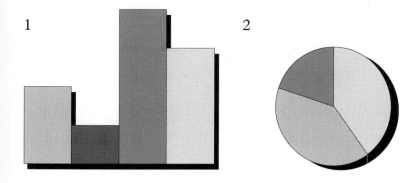

1   2

Follow-Up Activities

1 Choose a graph to explain – either from your own work or from the business press.

2 How are statistics presented in your company?

3 How can computers help to display data effectively? (graphics/screen displays/spreadsheets)

4 Can we be sure that statistics are always accurate and up-to-date or can they sometimes present rather a false picture?

5 Statistics are becoming more and more important in the modern business world. Do we rely too heavily on them?

Import/Export

Here are eight documents that are used for import/export.
Look at the descriptions and identify each one.

e.g. 1= *d* standard shipping note

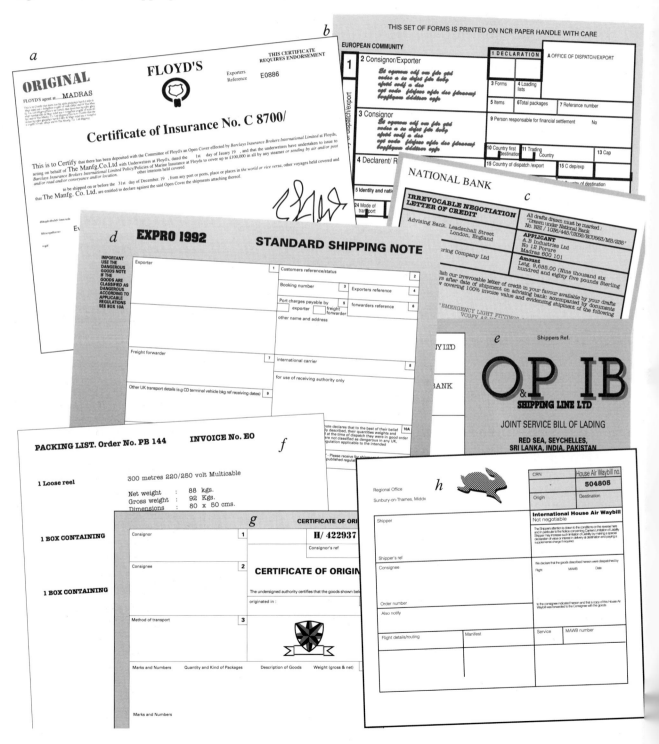

a

ORIGINAL

FLOYD'S agent at..... MADRAS

FLOYD'S

Exporters
Reference   E0886

THIS CERTIFICATE
REQUIRES ENDORSEMENT

Certificate of Insurance No. C 8700/

This is to Certify that there has been deposited with the Committee of Floyd's an Open Cover effected by *Barclays Insurance Brokers International Limited* at Floyds,
acting on behalf of The Manfg.Co.Ltd with Underwriters at Floyd's, dated the   1st   day of Janury 19   , and that the underwriters have undertaken to issue to
Barclays Insurance Brokers International Limited Policy/Policies of Marine Insurance at Floyds to cover up to £100,000 in all by any steamer or sending by air and/or post
and/or road and/or conveyance and/or location.   other interests held covered and

that The Manfg. Co. Ltd.   to be shipped on or before the   31st day of December. 19   , from any port or ports, place or places in *the world or vice versa*, other voyages held covered and
are entitled to declare against the said Open Cover the shipments attaching thereof.

b

THIS SET OF FORMS IS PRINTED ON NCR PAPER HANDLE WITH CARE

EUROPEAN COMMUNITY

1	2 Consignor/Exporter		1 DECLARATION	A OFFICE OF DISPATCH/EXPORT
			3 Forms	4 Loading lists
	3 Consignor		5 Items	6 Total packages	7 Reference number
		9 Person responsable for financial settlement		No
	4 Declarent/R	10 Country first destination	11 Trading Country	13 Cap
		15 Country of dispatch /export	15 C dep/exp	
	5 Identity and natio			Country of destination
	24 Mode of transport			

c

NATIONAL BANK

**IRREVOCABLE NEGOTIATION
LETTER OF CREDIT**

Advising Bank. Leadenhall Street
London, England

....ring Company Ltd

...lish our irrevocable letter of credit in your favour available by your drafts
...ys after date of shipment on advising bank: accompanied by documents
...v covering 100% invoice value and evidencing shipment of the following

"EMERGENCY LIGHT FITTINGS..
VCQFV A.S...

All drafts drawn must be marked :
"Drawn under National Bank
No. NBI / 1036/445/UK56/ECU663/MB/235"

APPLICANT
A.B Industries Ltd
No 12 Porure
Madras 600 101

Amount
Lstg. 9,685.00 (Nine thousand six
hundred and eighty five pounds Sterling

d

EXPRO 1992

STANDARD SHIPPING NOTE

IMPORTANT
USE THE
DANGEROUS
GOODS NOTE
IF THE
GOODS ARE
CLASSIFIED AS
DANGEROUS
ACCORDING TO
APPLICABLE
REGULATIONS
SEE BOX 10A

Exporter		1	Customers reference/status		2
			Booking number	3	Exporters reference	4
			Port charges payable by exporter ☐ freight ☐ forwarder	5	forwarders reference	6
			other name and address		
Freight forwarder		7	international carrier		8
			for use of receiving authority only		
Other UK transport details (e.g CD terminal vehicle bkg ref receiving dates)		9			

...note declares that to the best of their belief
...ly described, their quantities weights and
...at the time of dispatch they were in good order
...are not classified as dangerous in any UK,
...egulation applicable to the intended

10A

- Please receive for shippmen..
..published regula...

e

O&P IB

Shippers Ref.

SHIPPING LINE LTD

JOINT SERVICE BILL OF LADING

**RED SEA, SEYCHELLES,
SRI LANKA, INDIA, PAKISTAN**

...Y LTD

...BANK

f

PACKING LIST. Order No. PB 144   INVOICE No. EO

1 Loose reel   300 metres 220/250 volt Multicable

Net weight   :   88 kgs.
Gross weight :   92 Kgs.
Dimensions   :   80 x 50 cms.

1 BOX CONTAINING

1 BOX CONTAINING

g

CERTIFICATE OF ORI...

Consignor	1
Consignee	2
Method of transport	3
Marks and Numbers	Quantity and Kind of Packages	Description of Goods	Weight (gross & net)

H/ 422937

Consignor's ref

CERTIFICATE OF ORIGIN

The undersigned authority certifies that the goods shown bel...
originated in :

Marks and Numbers

h

| | CRN | House Air Waybill no. |
| Regional Office
Sunbury-on-Thames, Middx | - | **504805** |
| | Origin | Destination |
| Shipper | **International House Air Waybill**
Not negotiable | |
| | The Shippers attention is drawn to the conditions on the reverse here
and in particular to the Notice containing Carriers Limitation of Liability
Shipper may increase such limitation of Liability by making a special
declaration of value or interest in delivery at destination and paying a
supplemental charge if required. | |
Shipper's ref		
Consignee	We declare that the goods described hereon were despatched by	
	Flight	MAWB	Date
Order number		
Also notify	to the consignee indicated hereon and that a copy of this House Air
Waybill was forwarded to the Consignee with the goods	
Flight details/routing	Manifest	Service	MAWB number

1 This form gives details of goods being shipped. e.g. standard shipping note

2 This form has to be filled in for the customs authorities.

3 This document ensures that the exporter will be paid.

4 This document is sent with the goods to show they have been checked.

5 This document is evidence that goods have been sent by air.

6 This document shows where goods come from.

7 This document is an agreement to insure the goods being exported.

8 This receipt is a document of title to goods which have been loaded on the ship.

---

3 Mr Rossi of Brevetti, Italy, imports computer equipment from Central Computers U.K. Here are ten stages in the importation process. Put them in the correct order.

a   sends fax to check availability of stock

b   receives Central Computers' invoice

c   bank issues irrevocable letter of credit

d   orders the computers

e   receives pro-forma invoice

f   selects computers from catalogue   e.g. | 1

g   receives confirmation of order

h   pays transporters

i   receives copy of bill of lading from transporters

j   receives merchandise with customs declaration form

---

4 There are four important abbreviations in import/export concerning price and responsibility. What do they stand for?

Look at this chart and mark with a cross what the exporter pays each time.

The price of goods includes:

e.g.

	1 f.a.s.	2 c. and f.	3 c.i.f.	4 f.o.b.
a packing ready for shipment	✗			
b delivery to quayside	✗			
c loading on ship				
d freight charges to named port of destination				
e insurance charges				

Follow-Up Activities

1 Describe in detail any import/export forms with which you are familiar.

2 Mistakes in documents hold up the movement of goods or payment. How can these be kept to a minimum?

3 In your experience of importing and exporting, what are the major difficulties?

4 Is there too much paperwork in import/export? Should it be simplified or does it provide a necessary guarantee at every stage of the operation?

5 A new system is being developed to send trade documents electronically instead of on paper. What do you see as the main advantages and disadvantages?

Insurance

Look at these twelve insurable risks and losses and match each picture
with the correct description.

e.g. 1 = legal expenses

- public liability • damage to stock •
- cost of changing locks following theft of keys •
- burglary and theft • goods in transit •
- cost of replacing glass in shop windows •
- legal expenses • product liability •

- cost of compiling computer records again if damaged •
- theft of money from premises • business interruption/consequential loss •
- employer's liability •

Complete this extract from a brochure promoting Rayne Insurance Services to potential business customers. The first letter and a definition are given to help you find the twelve missing words.

e.g. 1 = branches

RAYNE INSURANCE SERVICES has an extremely successful reputation and a vast network of b___(1)___ throughout the world. We have an annual p___(2)___ income of over £10 billion. Our business premises c___(3)___ is the most up-to-date and c___(4)___ available. Not only is it very flexible, but there are also optional extras to suit the specific requirements of all p___(5)___. If your business demands above-average insurance values, we offer special d___(6)___ on our very competitive r___(7)___. C___(8)___ are dealt with quickly and efficiently by our highly-trained staff who have many years of experience in b___(9)___ and u___(10)___. There is no r___(11)___ too heavy or l___(12)___ too great for Rayne to handle.

1 local offices
2 payment made by an individual or a business for insurance
3 guaranteed protection given by an insurance policy
4 which includes everything
5 people who have bought insurance from an insurance company
6 reductions in price
7 prices
8 applications to an insurance company to pay for loss or damage
9 buying and selling insurance
10 providing the money needed to meet the costs
11 possibility of loss or damage covered by insurance
12 that which has been lost

How much do you know about the people who work in insurance?
e.g. 1 = actuary

Agent

Adjuster

Assessor

Actuary

1 Who is employed by the insurance company to calculate the level of risk and therefore how much the premium will be?

2 Who works out how much will be paid by the insurance company to settle a claim?

3 Who sells insurance policies for one company normally working on commission?

4 Who does the same job as an assessor?

Follow-Up Activities

1 What kind of business or personal insurance do you have and what does it cover?

2 Have you ever made an insurance claim? Were you satisfied with the compensation you received?

3 With the increasing risks of modern life, should insurance be made compulsory for individuals as well as businesses?

4 What risks are not normally covered by insurance policies? (war damage, earthquake). Does this seems inevitable?

5 How does insurance encourage increased economic activity?

Telephoning

Choose words from the list to label these ten pictures.

e.g. 10 = phone card

2 _____

3 _____

1 _____

5 _____

4 _____

6 _____

10 _____

8 _____

7 _____

9 _____

directory	car phone	phone card	memory	pay phone
operator	handset	answer phone	switchboard	mobile phone

8

Read this newspaper article.

The Mobile Phone Market is Booming

There are now over one million telephone subscribers in the UK – the most in Europe.

But Scandinavians are the most enthusiastic mobile phone users. Almost one in a hundred Swedes has a mobile phone compared to one in five hundred for the UK. Elsewhere in Europe the use of the mobile phone has been limited.

The growth in the UK is partly due to its deregulated telecommunications market and the competition this introduced: at the moment, the cost of owning a portable phone in the UK is the cheapest in Europe. Using a portable phone in Sweden is more than twice as expensive as in the UK and in France and Germany it costs almost five times as much.

The introduction of mobile phones is slowly increasing around Europe. The German government has authorized a third cellular network to cope with new demand. In Italy a consortium is competing to provide the country's second system. It has been calculated there will be 30 million portable phones in use in Europe by the year 2000. In Eastern Europe the figure will be around 1.5 million.

Correct the false statements. Which of these statements are true according to the report?

1 The U.K. has the highest percentage of mobile phone users in Europe.

2 Mobile phones are more popular in Scandinavia than in EC countries.

3 Using a mobile phone in France is five times as expensive as in Sweden.

4 By the end of this century, there will be more than one million portable phones in Eastern Europe.

Now check that you know what these words mean by choosing the correct answer.

5 A telephone **subscriber** is
a a person who has a telephone
b a person who has shares in the telephone company
c a person who works in telecommunications

6 To **cope with** a demand is to
a meet and satisfy it
b to stimulate and encourage it
c to provide competition for it

7 When a market is **deregulated**
a a standard system has been imposed
b prices have been kept as low as possible
c government control has been reduced

8 A **consortium** is
a a group of companies in competition for a contract
b a state authority
c a group of companies working together

Here is a short telephone conversation between the receptionist at Burton Electrics and Mr Brad Barnes. Eight common words and phrases are missing. Try to decide what they are before you look at the list. e.g. 1 = Could I speak to

R: Hello. Burton Electrics.

BB: __(1)__ _____ _____ _____ Mr Evans please on __(2)__ 225.

R: Certainly. __(3)__ _____ a minute please. I'll __(4)__ _____ _____.
     (Short pause)

R: I'm sorry. His __(5)__ is __(6)__ . Would you like to __(7)__ _____ _____?

BB: Could you tell him that Brad Barnes of Inigo Incorporated called and ask him to __(8)__ _____ _____?

R: Certainly Mr Barnes. Thank you for calling. Goodbye.

line
put you through
Could I speak to
leave a message
call me back
Hold on
extension
engaged

Follow-Up Activities

1 Describe the kind of professional phone calls you generally make or receive.

2 What sort of telephone system do you have at your place of work? (switchboard/answer phones etc.)

3 Will mobile phones change the way we do business now?

4 Is business better served by a nationalized or private telephone service?

5 How do you see international telecommunications developing over the next ten years?

Computers

Label these ten items of computer hardware.

**portable computer   monitor   word processor   printer
external single disk drive   mouse   modem   keyboard
screen   personal computer**

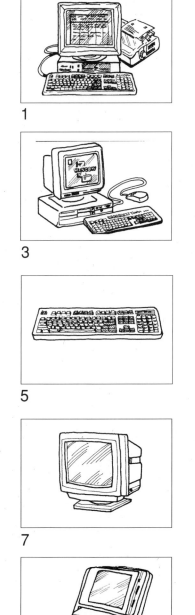

1

3

5

7

9

e.g. | 1 *word processor*

2

3

4

5

6

7

8

9

10

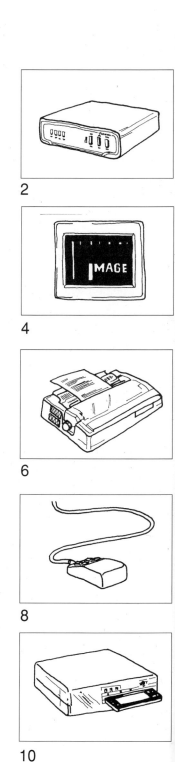

2

4

6

8

10

3 Three speakers are describing the equipment they each need. Choose words
from the list to complete their descriptions.
e.g. 1 = high resolution
3 ½"/high-resolution/compatible/high-level/dot matrix/upgradable/non-glare/laser/single/compact

Michael Riccioli, architect
"I want to buy a high-speed computer, so that I can get my reports finished quickly. I need
___(1)___ colour graphics to make my plans clear to the client. I have to use sophisticated programs so the
computer must work with ___(2)___ software. I need something with an ___(3)___ memory to make it easy
to expand the system."

Hilary Davies, sales representative
"I need a lightweight computer which I can travel with, which is ___(4)___ and can be easily carried on the
shoulder. It must be ___(5)___ with my office computer, and must work with a ___(6)___ printer as we need
very high quality printouts."

Ruben Greenberg, Harvard business student
"I don't want anything too complicated, a word processor with a ___(7)___ disk drive will do, for
___(8)___ disks. I must have a ___(9)___ screen so that my eyes don't get tired. I will also need a simple,
cheap, ___(10)___ printer."

One of the speakers chose this personal computer. By reading the technical specifications, try to work out
who it was.

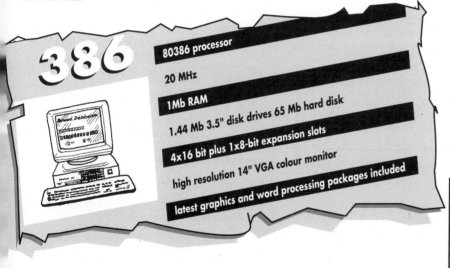

386

80386 processor

20 MHz

1Mb RAM

1.44 Mb 3.5" disk drives 65 Mb hard disk

4x16 bit plus 1x8-bit expansion slots

high resolution 14" VGA colour monitor

latest graphics and word processing packages included

Follow-Up Activities

1 Are you satisfied with the
   computer you have chosen?

2 Are you satisfied with the
   software?

3 How long did it take to learn
   to use your computer?

4 In what way could you
   improve your computer
   system?

5 A computer is only as good as
   its user and most people use
   only between 10% and 20% of
   a computer's potential. What
   can be done about this?

In computing, many vocabulary items are made up of two words
e.g. **data** + **base** = **database**. Here are some typical examples.

Which words go together?

micro	work
spread	processor
floppy	disk
print	sheet
lap	out
net	top

Recruitment

Job advertisements are often published in separate sections of newspapers and magazines, and use rather specialized vocabulary to describe both the position and the person they seek to recruit. Here are six job advertisements with extracts from six letters of application. Match each letter with the job it was written for.

1

LEGAL GRADUATE

Specialist European legal claims handling organization wishes to appoint in a marketing/technical role a legal graduate with good fluency in French and possibly one other European language.
The position is a new one to report to the Legal Manager. The candidate selected must be a self-starter and will be expected to develop existing contacts and to expand the account of existing contracts for the handling of multi-national legal disputes.

3

REGIONAL LEASING AND PERMITS ACCOUNT MANAGER

As part of the sales and marketing team at our national sales office, you will be responsible for recommending objectives for new and existing business and negotiating permits for leases with city building and planning departments. An advanced degree or MBA is a plus. Prospects are first class. Appointment carries potential for rapid promotion.

5

Administrator

London subsidiary of international French wine company offers opportunity to gain experience in accounts and administration. The successful applicant will possess good organisational skills and the ability to work under pressure. An eye for detail and sense of humour are essential. Typing skills and PC experience will be an advantage.
Assistance to study towards trade or other professional qualifications is available.

4

EUROPEAN SALES & MARKETING EXECUTIVE
STERILIZATION EQUIPMENT

You'll need to demonstrate good communication skills and an ability to negotiate in committee at senior level.
Salary depends on your experience and is complemented by attractive benifits including profit sharing, five weeks holiday and relocation assistance if appropiate.

6

CONFERENCE SECRETARY

We are looking for an efficient and highly motivated Administrative Secretary to help with the organisation and running of a major international conference.

The ideal candidate should have previous relevant experience including fast, accurate typing. Responsibilities will include liaison with speakers, travel and accommodation arrangements and preparing publicity material for publication.

2

Russian speaking export manager, London, Salary up to 25k + car. Large international organisation seeks experienced export area manager to expand in the U.S.S.R. Based in London, you will be travelling for up to 4 months a year, be responsible for business development and co-ordination of technical support staff. Fluent Russian and previous experience in export sales essential.

e.g. 4 = c

a I graduated from the University of Paris II in 1988 with a Masters degree in International Law and am at present working as a consultant for a publishing company specializing in English and French law textbooks for universities and colleges.

b Although my Public Relations experience is limited, I very much enjoy this kind of work and feel sure that with my studies of computing I can combine.

c I have a solid sales background with four years recent industrial experience (heavy equipment).

d At HyperRidd International I was involved in exporting alloys from the Ukraine to all parts of Europe and the Far East and worked closely with local suppliers.

e This will be my first job, but I was very active at college editing the school magazine, using a word processor and being responsible for the financial side as well.

f Last year I was responsible for presenting two projects to the city building department in New York and am now keen to extend my expertise in this field.

Complete these four vocabulary networks with the words and expressions that are underlined in the advertisements.

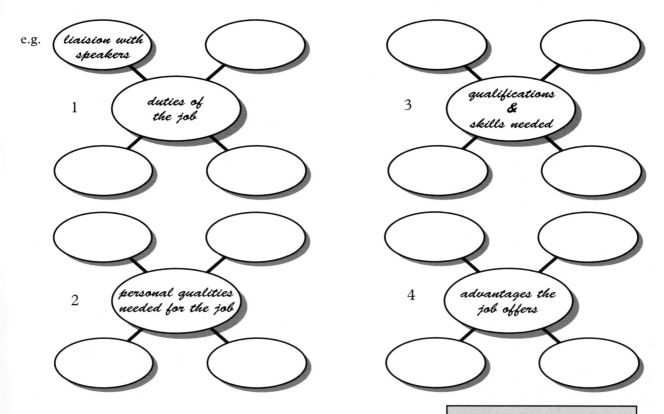

e.g.

1 — *liaision with speakers* — *duties of the job*

2 — *personal qualities needed for the job*

3 — *qualifications & skills needed*

4 — *advantages the job offers*

Choose words from the list to complete this newspaper advertisement.

competitive	ambitious	benefits	maximum
bonus	record	knowledge	communicator

e.g. 1 = ambitious

Leading Manufacturer Seeks European Sales Manager

* Must be an __(1)__ self-starter with a proven track __(2)__.
* Must have the ability to use time to __(3)__ effect.
* This is a demanding role for a gifted __(4)__ with a sound __(5)__ of German and Spanish.
* We offer a __(6)__ salary plus __(7)__ scheme and substantial __(8)__ package.

Follow-Up Activities

1 Explain how you found your present (and any previous) employment.

2 If you wanted to find a new job now, how would you go about it?

3 Write a job advertisement for your present position (including duties, advantages, personal qualities and professional skills).

4 It is now illegal in many countries to discriminate against candidates on the grounds of sex, race or disability. But how real are so-called equal job opportunities in your opinion?

5 Advertising a job in the newspaper is a risky business, but is it as risky as paying a headhunter or an agency? How can the risks be reduced and the right person for the job found more often?

13

Company Structure

Big companies employing a large workforce have complex internal structures, with separate specialist departments in charge of different functions. There are nine such departments at this company headquarters. Match each function with the department responsible for it.

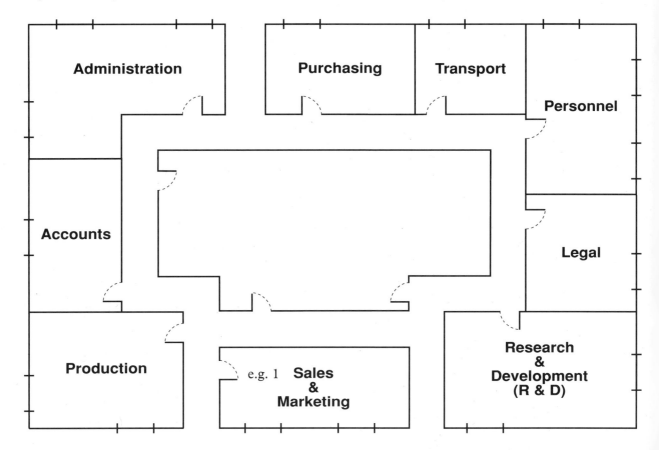

Ground Plan of Headquarters

Functions

1 carries out market research
2 works with the factory unit
3 runs the mail room for all incoming and outgoing correspondence
4 draws up contracts
5 operates the firm's lorries, vans and cars
6 works to improve the firm's product range
7 responsible for recruitment and selection
8 pays wages and salaries
9 in charge of the welfare of employees
10 includes data processing services
11 advises on corporate regulations
12 arranges delivery of goods to customers
13 organizes the activities of the sales representatives
14 provides office services, such as typing and photocopying
15 creates new products
16 keeps a record of all payments made and received
17 brings the firm's goods and services to the attention of potential customers
18 organizes training courses
19 orders all supplies needed by the firm
20 organizes quality control to maintain product standards

Complete this extract from one large company's annual report. There are twelve missing words and a choice of four possibilities for each.

Open communication with all employees is vital to achieving that sense of personal ___(1)___ in the company, without which our steady ___(2)___ would be impossible. ___(3)___ communication between management and employees has played a key role in building the excellent ___(4)___ relations on which we pride ourselves.

We recognise that professional enthusiasm does not depend solely on pay ___(5)___, but also on the opportunities employees have to participate in the ___(6)___ process and contribute to plans and choices that affect their jobs and careers.

All employees receive regular issues of our ___(7)___ magazine and information booklets on our ___(8)___ and plans, as well as regular ___(9)___ of progress.

Advance ___(10)___ of any changes to the business is given to all employees who may be affected. Managers meet on a ___(11)___ basis with elected staff ___(12)___ to tackle any problems and to ensure efficiency and stability.

e.g.

1 improvement / (involvement) / popularity / development

2 share / market / size / growth

3 specific / formal / face-to-face / accurate

4 labour / public / departmental / external

5 days / scales / claims / demands

6 training / promotion / decentralization / decision-making

7 popular / publicity / in-house / do-it-yourself

8 politics / policies / portfolio / prestige

9 programmes / levels / promises / reviews

10 notice / consideration / help / publication

11 freelance / quick / regular / standard

12 personnel / representatives / staff / executives

There are four main types of business ownership in the private sector of the economy: public limited company (PLC), partnership, sole trader & private limited company (Ltd.). Put each one into the correct box to complete the table.

1 Sole trader	2	3	4
one person provides all the capital	owned by two or more people who contribute capital	a registered company with restricted share transfer	a registered company whose shares can be bought and sold on the Stock Exchange
unlimited liability (the personal assets of the owner(s) can be taken to pay any business debts)		limited liability (liability for business debts is limited to the amount of capital subscribed)	

Follow-Up Activities

1 Describe the general organization of your company or one you know.

2 Choose two departments of a large company and describe their functions in detail.

3 What are the advantages of working for a smaller firm? (wider range of activities etc)

4 How is internal communication organized in your firm? And how could it be improved?

5 The type of business most likely to fail is that of the sole trader. Why should this be so?

Bank Forms

Here are six different forms commonly used in banking. Look at the situations below and say which form you would use for each.

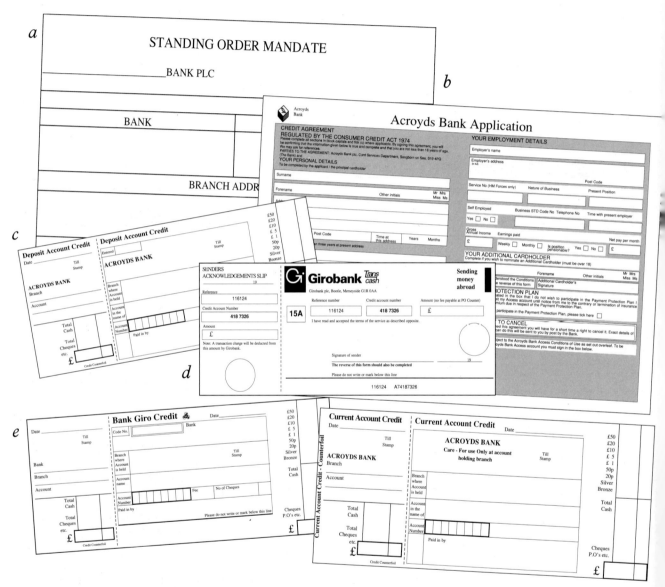

e.g. 1 = d

1 You need to pay money to someone overseas.

2 You want to pay money into a savings account.

3 You want to apply for a credit card.

4 You want to authorize regular payments of a set sum from one bank account to another.

5 You want to pay money into your personal cheque account.

6 You want to pay a bill directly into a creditor's account.

Card Application

Personal Details

1 Please complete all questions in ⬯ ballpoint or felt-tipped pen   ⬯ *MRS*

2 Forename(s) *DOROTHY ANN*

Surname *LLEWELLYN*

Address *31 LONDON ROAD*

BRIGHTON

3 County *SUSSEX*   ⬯ *BN1 23X*

4 Please ⬯ boxes where necessary   Own Home ☑   Tenant ☐   With Parents ☐   Years of Residence ☐

Full Phone No. *0273 660 3771*   Date of Birth *2 0 0 3 4 8*

Married ☐   Single ☐   Divorced ☑   Separated ☐

5 Primary use of the Card   Please send to: ⬯

Business ☑   Personal ☐   Home Address ☑   Office Address ☐

6 ⬯ Details

Bank Name *NAT. WESTMINSTER*

Address *14 MARINE PARADE*

BRIGHTON

SUSSEX

Postcode *BN2 4X*   Full Phone No. *0273 413866*

7 ⬯ | 3 | 0 | - | 8 | 0 | - | 4 | 0 |

Personal Current Account No. | 3 | 6 | 1 | 1 | 4 | 7 | 8 | | | |

8 Other Bank Accounts ⬯   ☑   Mortgage ☑   Joint ☐

Business Details

Employer's Name / Name of own Business

DALEY & LLEWELLYN

Address *14 HIGH STREET*

LINDFIELD, SUSSEX

Postcode *RH16 2QX*   Full Phone No *044 473122*

Employee number (if applicable)

9 ⬯ *LAND MANAGEMENT*

Years with employer or years of trading *5 YEARS*

10 My annual ⬯ is:

11 ⬯ held *SURVEYOR*   £ *25,000*

12 Are you: ⬯ ☑ retired ☐   of independent means ☐

13 If self-employed or of independent means, please give name and address of your ⬯ whom we may contact regarding your income.

MR C J PATEL

18 DAVIS AVENUE, HAYWARDS HEATH

Postcode *RH12 4B*   Full Phone No *044 455533*

14 Please ⬯ below

15 Please ⬯ you have completed all the details and sign here.

x   *D. A. Llewellyn*

Look at this credit card application form and put the fifteen missing words and phrases in the box below back in the right places.

e.g. 1 = Title

Nature of Business	check	block capitals
monthly statement	Title	Bank Sort Code
Position	Financial	accountant
tick	sign	Postcode
self-employed	income	Deposit

Follow-Up Activities

1 What sort of forms have you filled in recently? Choose two and explain how to complete them.

2 What is the best way to send money abroad?

3 What are the advantages of standing orders and direct debits to businesses?

4 We are constantly filling in forms in modern society. How could all this paperwork be reduced?

5 A great deal of the personal and professional information entered on forms is stored on large central computers. Do you think this is dangerous? How should it be controlled?

Correspondence

A

Here is a typical layout of a simple commercial letter. Use the twelve different parts shown to put together the letter below.

e.g. 12 = a

1	letterhead

2 references

3 date

4	addressee's name and address

5	salutation

6	subject title

7	body of letter

8	complimentary close

9	signature

10	company position

11	enclosures

12	copies

a c.c. Martin Naylor, International Holdings, Singapore

l Yours sincerely,

j J. Hardy

Janet Hardy

k 23 June 1992

i Dear Mr Mexford,

c Enc. Managing Director's itinerary

b Due to a change of programme, Mr Gilbert Smethers will now be arriving in Singapore on 18 July and not 16 July as originally planned. Would it be convenient to re-schedule your meeting with him for 19 July at 10.30 a.m.? Please contact our agent, Martin Naylor, to confirm that this is possible or to suggest an alternative time.

h

g Mr Alan Mexford, Financial Consultant, 2 Victoria Buildings, New Bridge Road, Singapore

d Our ref: JH/298

Personal Assistant to the Managing Director

f **International Holdings PLC**

Nelson House, Grosvenor Street, London W1X 9FH Tel: 071–444-2121 Fax: 071-443-0896 Telex: 514050

e *Visit of Mr Gilbert Smethers, Managing Director, International Holdin*

How much do you know about business mail? Try this quiz.

	True	False	Corrections and explanations
1 It is more polite to use **Sir** or **Madam** rather than the e.g. name of the person you are writing to.		✗	*If you know the name, you should always use it.*
2 **Ms** is used when you are writing to more than one woman.			
3 **Mister** is more correct than the abbreviated form **Mr**.			
4 In the U.S.A. a letter to a company usually starts with **Gentlemen:** and not **Dear Sirs**.			
5 If a customer uses a business reply service envelope, the postage is paid by the trader.			
6 **PLC** (Public Limited Company) is used in the U.S.A. instead of **Ltd**.			
7 The date is written differently in British and American letters.			
8 A letter that starts **Dear Sir** or **Dear Madam** will close with **Yours sincerely**.			
9 **p.p.** is used when someone signs a letter on behalf of someone else.			
10 The recorded delivery service provides proof of delivery and pays compensation if a valuable document is lost.			

Complete these eight stages in the letter-writing process.
The first letter of each verb is given to help you.

The letter is

  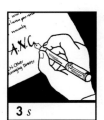 

| 1 *dictated* | 2 *t* | 3 *s* | 4 *f* |

The envelope is

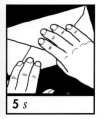   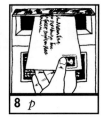

| 5 *s* | 6 *a* | 7 *s* | 8 *p* |

Follow-Up Activities

1 Give some examples of the type of business letters you send or receive in English.

2 How is incoming and outgoing mail dealt with at your place of work?

3 Should commercial correspondence be brief, business-like and to the point, or do you think that style and presentation are also important?

4 Each country has its own style of business correspondence. What comparisons can you make from your own experience?

5 **My word is my bond**. Is this still true of the spoken word in business or does only the written word give an absolute commitment?

Marketing

What are the four words beginning with **p** in the marketing mix? The number of
letters and an explanation are given to help you find them.

1 **p** _ _ _ _ _ _ (the item made for sale)

2 **p** _ _ _ _ (how much it will cost)

3 **p** _ _ _ _ _ _ _ _ (what publicity it will get)

4 **p** _ _ _ _ (where it will be sold)

This diagram shows the marketing process from start to finish. Insert the six
missing words in their correct positions.

research   distribution   strategy   consumer   costing   development

e.g. 5 = research

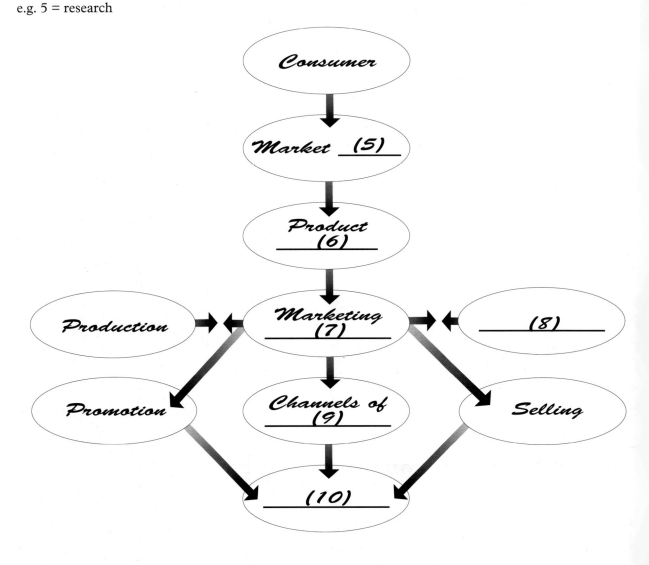

20

Packaging is an important part of marketing. Read this article and match each sentence on the right with the same idea in the text. The answer to number one has been underlined

e.g.

Packaging design

1 Besides protecting the product and making it easier to handle, manufacturers and retailers attach great importance to <u>packaging as a means to lure shoppers.</u> For example, Griffin's steak pie was recently re-designed – same contents and box, just different graphics – and, with subsequent marketing and promotion, sales reportedly went up 200 per cent.

For different types of product, different types of design may be more appropriate: toiletries are not quickly thrown away so their design may be more stylish than, say, baked beans which are kept in a cupboard. Packaging does have one basic design principle, though: it should stand out on the shop shelves. Designed with flair, it can promote the quality of a product.

1 Packaging can attract consumers and encourage them to buy.

2 Products that are used for a long time are worth smarter packaging than goods that are stored out of sight.

3 Packaging can prevent damage to the goods inside.

4 The best packaging not only says what is inside it, but also suggests how good the product is.

5 The fundamental rule about packaging is that it should be seen clearly in the shop.

Now find the words that correspond to these definitions (They are in the same order in the text).

6 changed

7 what is inside something

8 drawings and pictures

Labels can give the consumer quite a lot of information about a product. Which of the following are on this cheese packet label?

e.g. 1 = Lancashire (a type of cheese)

GRIFFINS Lancashire

£1.58	25SEP
PRICE PER LB	BEST BEFORE
lb WEIGHT oz	PACK PRICE
0 7⅜	£ 0.73

Keep refrigerated

0 317600 083078

1 the type of product

2 the name of the retailer

3 the weight of the item

4 the price the shopper pays

5 the bar code

6 instructions on how to store it

7 instructions on how long to keep it

8 a price given for the purposes of comparison with similar products

Follow-Up Activities

1 Find a selection of labels and explain the information given on each one.

2 Choose two examples of what you consider to be good packaging and say why.

3 Is cheapness always the best selling point?

4 Marketing aims to sell a company's products. Does it also serve the customer in any way?

5 Market research can be a long and expensive process. Why is it so necessary? Is it not possible to create a demand for a new product rather than trying to cater for an existing demand?

Transport

Containerization has streamlined the whole system of transporting goods. These pictures show the final stages in the delivery of a cargo of tropical fruit to the retailer. Match each sentence with the correct picture and choose word(s) from the list to fill in the gaps.

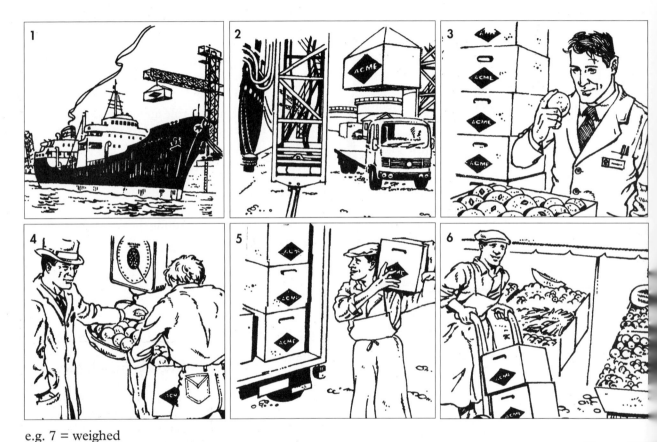

e.g. 7 = weighed

Picture No

a The fruit is __(7)__, graded and __(8)__ into cartons.

b The fruit is finally delivered to a variety of __(9)__ and markets.

c Once the ship has __(10)__ at the discharge __(11)__, the __(12)__ are taken out of the __(13)__ of the vessel by gantry cranes.   e.g. 1

d The __(14)__ are loaded onto vans for __(15)__.

e Once the containers reach the distribution centre, they are opened and a __(16)__ team conducts a __(17)__.

f The containers are moved around the port by straddle carriers and then loaded onto __(18)__.

packed	retail outlets	lorries	distribution
cartons	quality control	port	random check
weighed	hold	containers	docked

Each company has to choose the most suitable form of transport for its own needs. Here are some advantages and disadvantages of road, rail and air transport. Put each item into the correct box to complete the table.

- reduced insurance costs due to shorter transit time
- door-to-door service
- fastest over long distances
- not tied to any timetable
- no need for transhipment
- routes limited by lines and stations
- good for bulk commodities in large quantities
- most economical on fuel
- especially suitable for containers
- delayed by traffic congestion in cities
- weight and size of cargo limited
- can reach places inaccessible to other forms of transport
- high freight rates

e.g.

1 Road: advantages	2 Rail: advantages	3 Air: advantages
		• *reduced insurance costs due to shorter transit time*
4 Road: disadvantages	5 Rail: disadvantages	6 Air: disadvantages

If you heard the following comments, which of the three forms of transport would the people be talking about?

e.g. 1 = road transport

1

> The roll–on roll–off facilities mean the carrier doesn't have to unload in transit.

4

> I sent the coal that way as it was cheaper.

2

> We'd received an S.O.S. for the drugs so I didn't hesitate.

5

> The high–speed container service operates mainly at night when there is much less traffic on the lines.

3

> Of course it's even faster now there's the new motorway.

6

> We try to make sure the lorry has a fresh load for the return journey to keep haulage costs low.

Follow-Up Activities

1 Which form of transport does your company use most frequently? Are you satisfied with the service?

2 What criteria should businesses keep in mind when choosing a form of transport?

3 Containerization is becoming more and more widespread. What are its advantages and disadvantages?

4 Certain commodities (such as gas and oil) can be moved from one place to another by pipelines. Is this a more efficient and environment-friendly solution?

5 With the growing pressure on transport systems, which alternative methods could be revived or developed? (canals/rivers etc)

Business Mail

Here are the contents of a typical business mail box. Identify the ten items on the list.

chairman's statement / invoice / price list / statement of account / registration form / report / admission card / mail shot / periodical / subscription offer

e.g. 1 = chairman's statement

1

This statement sets out the results for the Group for the year which ended on 31 March 1992 and provides shareholders with the earliest possible information on the progress and development of the business.

The Annual Report and Accounts will be posted on 25 June 1992 and will be submitted to shareholders for approval at the Annual General Meeting on 28 July 1992.

2

PRACTICAL INFORMATION

The seminar will be conducted in **English** with simultaneous interpretation into **German** and **French.**

The price per participant is BF 25,000 (including VAT). This includes participation at the seminar, the luncheon, as well as pre-seminar documents and a book to be published shortly afterwards containing both the study and seminar proceedings.

NAME:...

POSITION:..

ORGANIZATION:...

ADDRESS:..

3

EUROPEAN
FINANCIAL
MARKET REVIEW

4

CARD B

Please bring this card with you when you come to the Meeting.

DR RICHARD MICHAEL GRIFFIN

This card shows that you are entitled to attend the Annual General Meeting.

5

Stk No cases pbc Clb Zalc/06			Commercial Description	LTS/LOA	HMC	Val ins Val
905070A	1	12	75.00	CH DU PAPE 86			
905070B	1	12	75.00	CH BONTISSE 1985	9.00	136.00	149.60
905070C	1	12	75.00	COTES DU RHONE	9.00	136.00	149.60
905070D	1	12	75.00	CORNAS ROUGE 1985	9.00	136.00	149.60
905070E	1	12	75.00	SAUTERNES LER CRU 85	9.00	136.00	149.60
905070F	2	12	75.00	LYNCH BAGES 1985	9.00	136.00	149.60
905070G	1	12	75.00	CH LANESSAN MEDOC 1985	18.00	136.00	149.60
905070H	1	12	75.00	CH LA CROIT DE GAY FOMEROL 85	9.00	136.00	149.60
905070J	1	12	75.00	CH SOCIANDO MALLET HAUT MEDOC 85	9.00	136.00	149.60

10 CASES

90.00 LITRES

PRIVATE WAREHOUSE RENT PER MONTH to 30 JUNE 1990
10 CASES 1 MONTHS @ £.38 per case/month
RECEIVING HOUSING & DELIVERY TO VAN   S   £3.80
10 CASES @ £1.35 per case
TRANSPORT COLLECTION CHARGES   S   £13.50
10 CASES @ £1.23 per case
INSURANCE is based on values given per case   S   £12.30
Goods Value £1,496.00 @ £1.00 % p.a. for 12 month(s)   Z   £14.96
VAT @ 15.00%   £4.44

PAYABLE 30 DAYS   £49.00

Now answer these questions.

1 Which five invite some sort of response? _____e.g. 2_____ _____ _____ _____ _____
2 Which three involve sending money? _____ _____ _____
3 Which five are for information? _____ _____ _____ _____ _____
4 Which two are financial records? _____ _____

6

INTRODUCTORY OFFER

Save up to 30% off the cover

I wish to take out a subscription for the time under the terms of your guarantee. As a new subscriber, you will be entitled

Please send this entire form, to (PO) Box 22, Harefield Road, Watford

Name Mr/Mrs/Miss _____

Initials _____

Job Title _____

Company _____

8

BACKGROUND REPORT
THE EUROPEAN COMMUNITY'S ENVIRONMENT POLICY

INTRODUCTION

World concern for the protection of the environment began to develop in the early 1970's. United Nations Conference on the Environment in Stockholm in 1972 called attention to the concerted action. The European Community response was to develop the principles of a Co environment policy, which led to four successive Community Action Programmes. The principle policy, defined in October 1972, was that pollution should be prevented at source to remedy its effect, that environment policy must be compatible with development, that environmental considerations must be taken into account and that polluters must pay.

The first Community Action Programme

7

AG10
SALE PRICE. £695 + VAT.
RENTAL PRICE. £120 + VAT PER (QTR).

AG20
SALE PRICE. £995 + VAT.
RENTAL PRICE. £125 + VAT PER QTR.

RD70
SALE PRICE. £995 + VAT
RENTAL PRICE. £140 + VAT PER QTR.

10

The Business Centre

SERVICES AVAILABLE

EFFECTIVE FROM THE 1ST MARCH 1990

TELEPHONE ANSWERING

Our telephone number can be printed on your stationery. All incoming telephone calls are answered with the telephone number and callers need not be aware or advised that you are not resident at the office. Telephone calls received out of office hours are recorded by automatic answering equipment You may telephone in for your messages, call in and collect them, or they can be relayed by telephone at times to suit you. Alternatively your own number can terminate in our reception we will answer using your correct Company title or trading name. In certain areas a 'Subscriber Controlled Transfer' system can be installed in conjunction with Telecom.

MAILING ADDRESS

You may use our address and print it on your headed notepaper together with your company name. Letters are held for your collection or will be posted on daily by first class mail according to your instructions.

TELEX

We offer a telex service for a fraction of the cost of maintaining an 'inhouse' facility, with no loss of efficiency. You may quote your telex number on your stationary and advertising literature. Outgoing telexes can be

9

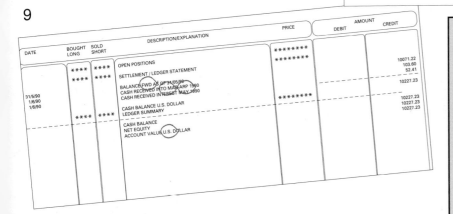

The following abbreviations have been circled in the documents.
Write them out in full. The context will help you.
e.g. 1 = Belgian francs

1	BF	4	@	7	PO	10	MAR
2	VAT	5	p.a.	8	qtr	11	APR
3	No	6	%	9	fwd	12	U.S.

Follow-Up Activities

1 What sort of mail do you ignore or throw away?

2 What sort of mail do you circulate to other offices?

3 Do you contact companies who send you mail shots, or do you prefer companies you know?

4 Collect some samples of business mail and explain how you would deal with them.

5 The increasing amount of material sent through the post indiscriminately is sometimes referred to as **junk mail**. Should it be more carefully targeted and controlled?

Career Profiles

Here are the details from Nigel Dolman's curriculum vitae. Use the layout below to put it together.

e.g. 1 = e

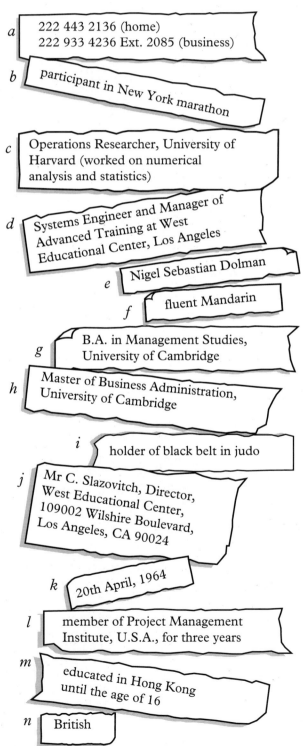

a 222 443 2136 (home)
222 933 4236 Ext. 2085 (business)

b participant in New York marathon

c Operations Researcher, University of Harvard (worked on numerical analysis and statistics)

d Systems Engineer and Manager of Advanced Training at West Educational Center, Los Angeles

e Nigel Sebastian Dolman

f fluent Mandarin

g B.A. in Management Studies, University of Cambridge

h Master of Business Administration, University of Cambridge

i holder of black belt in judo

j Mr C. Slazovitch, Director, West Educational Center, 109002 Wilshire Boulevard, Los Angeles, CA 90024

k 20th April, 1964

l member of Project Management Institute, U.S.A., for three years

m educated in Hong Kong until the age of 16

n British

o 1206 West 5th Street, Los Angeles, CA 90017 U.S.A.

p single

1	name
2	address
3	telephone
4	date of birth
5	nationality
6	marital status
7	education
8	present position
9	previous employment
10	membership of professional bodies
11	other skills + interests
12	referees

Read this article about a successful businesswoman. Find words in the text that mean the same as these five words (they are in order)

e.g. 1 = awards   1 prizes   2 contest   3 rivals   4 grow   5 activities

WOMAN CHAMPION

In May, the London Business Centre will be hosting the finale of the Women in Business Awards competition and Sally Cross, the reigning champion, will be there to inspire others with her own dynamic story.

After losing her job at the age of 35, Ms Cross took over her father's small air freight delivery service and started by putting up posters all over the area, offering fares that competitors could not match. She used her redundancy pay to purchase another light aircraft and with her enterprise and energy the business began to expand.

Soon she was able to buy up other companies and the operations of Cross Cargos Ltd. now extend throughout the whole country.

Now find the **odd man out**. Which of the three words is different in meaning?

6 fare   trip   excursion

7 cut-price   buy up   cheaper

8 job loss   dividend   redundancy

9 enterprise   genius   initiative

10 poster   advertisement   highlight

Three people have decided to advertise themselves in the newspaper in the hope of attracting prospective employers.

a

e.g.

YOUNG MANAGER

33 years old. Seeks new challenge.
Retail experience. Excellent leader.
Fast and decisive.
Highly literate. Able to work independently.
Entrepreneurial experience.
Will work on a performance related basis.

SPAIN CONSTRUCTION PROJECT MANAGER

Very fluent, last 15 years in Spain,
highly experienced, "hands on", owners
representative,
all forms of major projects, £5 –20 million.
Available for executive position
in Spain, Europe or South America.

b

c

ENTREPRENEUR SEEKS NEW CHALLENGE

39 years old, specializing in property, marketing, management and training, sold own business,
experienced small/large organizations.
Creative thinker with exceptional motivational skills. Will discuss any position.
Miss this opportunity at your peril!

1 Who is interested in selling to the public?

2 Who wants to work abroad?

3 Who was his own boss?

4 Who deals with buying and selling houses, offices and flats?

5 Who emphasises the practical nature of his experience?

6 Who is used to dealing with large sums of money?

7 Who has used humour in the advertisement?

8 Who is happy to relate salary to work output?

e.g. | *a* |
|---|
| |
| |
| |
| |
| |
| |
| |

Underline the part of the text that supports your answer.

Fax

Finish labelling this fax machine by inserting names of the following four parts in the boxes.

dialling keys / 10 sheet automatic document feeder / 16 digit liquid crystal display / up to A4 width scanning

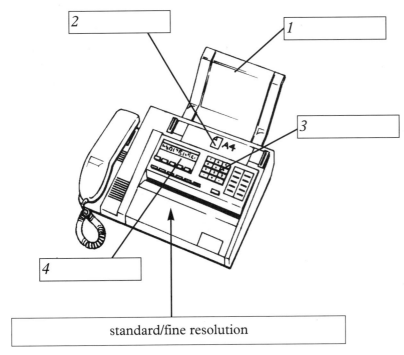

features summary

a   50 number memory

b   10 sheet automatic document feeder

c   50 metre paper roll

d   timer transmission

e   choice of standard or fine resolution settings

f   automatic redial

g   voice contact facility

h   16 digit LCD display

standard/fine resolution

5   Do you know what **fax** is an abbreviation for?

Here are eight questions people ask about fax machines. The machine described above can do everything they need. Which feature tells us that each time?

e.g. 1 = *c*

1

I receive documents 24 hours a day, often up to a hundred pages. Is there a machine that can do this when the office is closed?

2

Can I check that the fax has been received, and discuss the contents?

3

I have regular customers and numbers I use a lot, can the machine help me to dial them more quickly?

Here are five simple instructions for a typical fax transmission.
Use numbers to put them in the correct order.

e.g. 1 = e

Transmission will automatically be cancelled
when the fax has gone through.

Press **START.**

If the fax has not gone through and
you wish to try again, press **REDIAL.**

Dial the full fax number using the
numeric keys (key pad). If you dial a wrong
number, just press **STOP** and dial again.

Insert original(s)
face down.

Follow-Up Activities

1 Explain how to send a fax.

2 Has fax made (Would fax
   make) any difference to your
   way of working?

3 What advantages does fax
   have compared to telex?

4 Fax is now widespread in the
   business world. Will it ever
   replace the postal system for
   professional users?

5 Does fax make it too easy to
   send unnecessary and
   irrelevant documentation?

Bank Cards

A If all the plastic money cards in the U.K. were laid end to end, they would stretch from the doors of the Bank of England to the shores of Africa!

Do you know all the signs and symbols on a bank card? Match the eight details on the card below with the corresponding explanation.

e.g 1 = *e*

a Your current account number. All your card transactions will be debited to this account.

b "Valid From" date. Your card is valid from the first day of the month shown.

c Cheque guarantee limit. Your card will have one of two logos, which indicates the amount up to which a cheque for an individual transaction can be guaranteed.

d The Sorting Code of your current account holding branch.

e Your card number, which you will need to quote for mail order or telephone ordering.

f "Expires End" date. Your card is no longer valid for use after the last day of the month shown.

g Magnetic strip, which contains your card details and allows it to be used in cash dispensers and other electronic terminals.

h Your name. Please check the embossing for correctness.

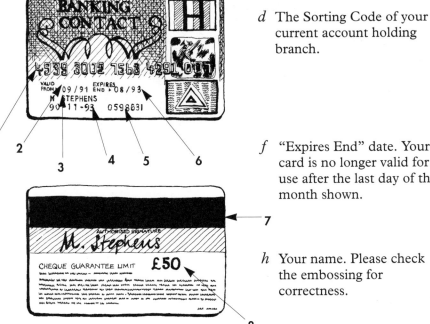

When you use your card to pay for goods or services, you are asked to sign a completed sales voucher. Look at this example and answer the questions.

9   What is the name of the cardholder?

10 How much did the cardholder spend?

11 When was the money spent?

12 Where was the money spent?

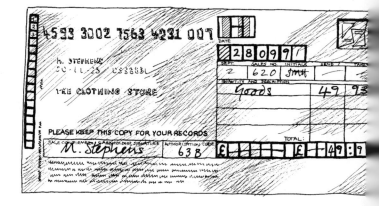

Put the following twelve sentences under the correct headings to complete the information summary.

a Notify the bank immediately.
b Insert your card.
c Never leave your card unattended in a car.
d Tap in your Personal Identification Number (PIN).
e Always keep your card separate from your cheque book.
f Confirm in writing within seven days.
g You can use it to withdraw cash from many banks worldwide.
h If you find your card again, cut it in half and return it to the bank.
i You can use it to withdraw cash from cash dispensers.
j You can use it to order over the phone.
k Memorize your PIN and never keep it with your card.
l Collect money and card.

THE FACTS ABOUT CARDS

1. Why a card is convenient.

☐ You can use it like a cheque but without having to carry a cheque book.
☐
☐
g. ☐ You can use it to order over the phone.

2. How to use cash dispensers.

☐
☐
☐ Tap in the amount of money you require.
☐

3. How to safeguard your card.

☐
☐ Always keep your card secure in your wallet or handbag.
☐
☐

4. What to do if you lose your card.

☐
☐
☐ Give the bank all the information about the loss or theft.
☐

Try this quiz. Look at the possibilities and choose the correct one.

1 Debit cards – like credit cards/payment cards/charge cards – do not allow a period of credit.

2 In America there are reputedly enough money cards in circulation for every person to have 2/6/18.

3 Bank cards are legally the property of the cardholder/the bank/the government.

Follow-Up Activities

1 How could the plastic cards you have fill your needs better?

2 Do you know what they cost?

3 What do you risk if they go astray?

4 What difference would it make to your life if you had to do without your cards?

5 As card technology advances and paper transactions are phased out, what sort of problems could we all face in the future?

Advertising

A If a retail chain is to maintain its profits, it is essential that stock moves in and out of store quickly. Here department store personnel are discussing the eight different ways of encouraging turnover listed below. Which is each person talking about? Fill in the spaces.

introductory offers   money-off coupons   competitions   jingles
free samples   gimmicks   demonstrators   window display

e.g. 3 = gimmicks

We could get in product ___(8)___ who would draw the crowds. They could give away ___(7)___ of products

Repeating ___(1)___ with intermittent soft music are what people are most influenced by, in my opinion

I am in favour of ___(2)___ because we can advertise the prizes all over the shops

We want something unsual to make our stores different from others, ___(3)___ are a good idea, ballons, stickers, ball point pens and so on

I think frequent ___(6)___ changes are a good bet. For example, bedrooms one week bathrooms, etc

What about having ___(4)___ on all new own brand lines for a period of a week, say a 5% or a 10% discount

Couldn't we concentrate more on our own-brand goods and provide ___(5)___, so that people will return to our shops

3 Identify the five key advertising media pictured here.

These eight verbs are commonly used in advertising. Choose the right one to complete each sentence.   e.g. 1 = appeal

attract   spend   promote   appeal
boost   launch   persuade   project

1 The copywriter created a slogan which would _____ to a wide cross-section of consumers.

2 The agency wants to _____ a campaign targeting the under-16 market.

3 The consumers we want to _____ are professionals who purchase up-market products.

4 All advertising must _____ the right product image.

5 Giving away free badges helped to _____ ice-cream sales to children.

6 The number of TV commercials in a campaign depends on how much the client wants to _____ and who he wants to reach.

7 The function of advertising is primarily to inform and to _____.

8 Our plan is to _____ the new product across a wide range of media.

Follow-Up Activities

1 What advertisements have caught your eye recently? Explain why you consider them to be successful.

2 Describe any good advertising gimmicks you have seen. What sort of impact did they have?

3 How do you see the promotion of merchandise by in-store demonstrators? What makes a good demonstration?

4 What do you think are the benefits of international product standardization?

5 Advertising can influence people's behaviour, sometimes – as in the case of the anti-smoking campaign – with very positive results. In what other fields could advertising play a beneficial role?

Car Hire

Renting a car is a feature of many business trips, both at home and abroad. Compare the services provided by Cars Unlimited and The Business Driver's Fleet and complete the checklist below.

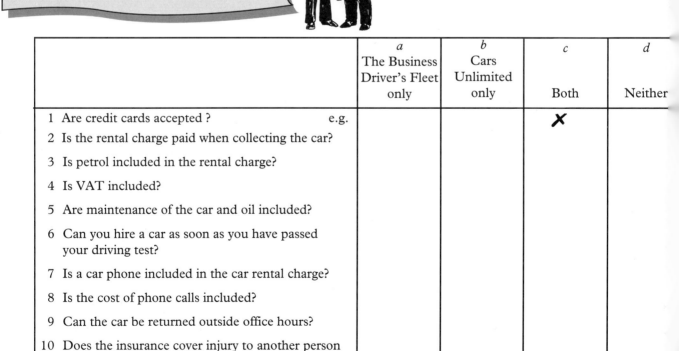

CARS UNLIMITED
TERMS AND CONDITIONS

RATES These are special rates applying to the rental branch. Not included is petrol, personal accident insurance cover, Collision Damage Waiver or VAT. Rates do include 24 hour breakdown cover, mainten-ance and oil. Rates may be subject to change or withdrawal without notice.

DRIVERS British drivers must produce a full current driving licence. Overseas visitors are required to produce a current driving licence valid in their own country. The driving licence must have been held for at least one year.

TELEPHONES Fitted to all cars – call charges extra.

INSURANCE Cover is provided against liability for an unlimited amount in respect of death or bodily injury to third parties. Damage to the property of the third parties is also covered up to a maximum of £500,000.

CARS Must be taken and returned by the hirer during branch business hours from and to branch from which rented within stipulated time limits.

PAYMENT Payment may be either by cheque or credit card. Charges will be computed at end of rental by the renting branch.

The Business Driver's Fleet
HIRING INFORMATION

CAR TELEPHONES A transportable car telephone facility is available. Rental Charges as follows:

Daily Rental Charge: £7.50
Phone Units Charge: £0.40p

INSURANCE Rental rates include insurance which provides indemnity to all approved drivers against claims by third parties (including passengers), fire, theft and accidental damage.

PAYMENT The estimated cost of the Rental is payable at the commencement of the hire. Cheques can only be accepted when accompanied by a bankers card or by prior arrangement. Credit cards can be used as part or full payment.

DRIVING LICENCE A full valid driving licence must be produced by each driver at the time of rental. A driver must have at least 12 months driving experience on a full licence. Endorsements may be accepted at the Company's discretion. Overseas visitors must produce a licence valid in their country and, where appropriate, an international driving permit.

RETURNING THE VEHICLE The hirer may return the vehicle at any time between 08.30 and 23.00 hours. Any money due to be refunded will be forwarded by post or can be collected the following day.

RATES Rates include fully comprehensive insurance of the vehicle, VAT, maintenance and oil. Rates do not include petrol.

	a The Business Driver's Fleet only	b Cars Unlimited only	c Both	d Neither
1 Are credit cards accepted ? e.g.			✗	
2 Is the rental charge paid when collecting the car?				
3 Is petrol included in the rental charge?				
4 Is VAT included?				
5 Are maintenance of the car and oil included?				
6 Can you hire a car as soon as you have passed your driving test?				
7 Is a car phone included in the car rental charge?				
8 Is the cost of phone calls included?				
9 Can the car be returned outside office hours?				
10 Does the insurance cover injury to another person and damage to another car?				

3 One customer found the service provided by The Business Driver's Fleet to be very unsatisfactory. Read the letter of complaint and use the information to fill in the Service Evaluation form. Underline the relevant parts of the letter. The first question on the form has been done for you.

SERVICE EVALUATION

We at The Business Driver's Fleet want our customers to be perfectly satisfied.
Your comments will help us to ensure this. Please indicate YES or NO as appropriate and add any additional comments you may wish to make. Thank you very much for your co-operation in this matter.

	Comments	YES	NO
1 The vehicle was received on time.	*20 minutes late*		✗
2 The vehicle was damage free.			
3 The vehicle was in good mechanical condition.			
4 The vehicle was clean inside and outside.			
5 The staff were helpful and efficient.			
6 The vehicle controls were explained.			
7 The office was convenient and well-run.			
8 The invoicing system was efficient.			

Although I had notified the company that I would be in a hurry, I was kept waiting for twenty minutes because no cars were available. The one that was eventually found for me was an impressive-looking car with an impressive-looking range of instruments; it was unfortunate that I had no idea how to use many of them. My client enjoyed the smooth ride, but found her ashtray to be already full of ash, which did not give quite the impression I wished to convey!

When I finally managed to find your office, the receptionist apologized but offered neither explanation nor refund. She could not even give me a proper invoice as the computer was out-of-order.

Follow-Up Activities

1 Describe what happened the last time you hired a car (for personal or professional purposes).

2 What criteria do you use when choosing a car hire firm?

3 In which countries have you driven a car? Were the driving conditions very different?

4 What action do you take if you are not satisfied with a service?

5 Would you agree that a car is an important business tool? Does it convey an image as much as provide a means of transport?

Conferences

The number of news items about conference speeches is a reflection of just how important meetings of this kind have become for the international business community. Read the information about this international conference and match Delegate Two's answers to Delegate One's questions/concerns.
e.g. 1 = *d*

Information

The language of the conference will be English.

The morning session on each day will commence at 09.00 and delegates are invited to collect their documents during the pre-forum reception from 19.00 to 21.00.

The registration fee of £650.00 is payable in advance and includes the cost of all refreshments, cocktails, lunches, receptions, documents and copies of speakers' papers. Discounts on the registration fee are given on corporate block bookings, details are available on request.

Fees (less a 10% administration charge) will be returned for any cancellation received before Wednesday, 30 March. However, substitutions are accepted at any time.

The fee does not include accommodation. A limited amount of accommodation is available at Lodge Hotel.

DELEGATE ONE

1 I don't know what to do about accommodation.
2 I hope we don't have to pay extra for meals.
3 How many languages will the conference be in?
4 I'd like Jim to go in my place if I can't attend.
5 I wonder when we stop for lunch.
6 I can't pay until the second day.
7 Can we collect our programme during the reception?
8 Perhaps it will be cheaper if we all pay at the same time.

DELEGATE TWO

a Yes we can between 7.00 p.m. and 9.00 p.m.
b They don't say.
c They ask for the fee before it starts.
d You might get a room at the conference hotel.
e There's no problem about that.
f Dinner isn't included, but otherwise food and drink is paid for.
g Only one.
h Let's ask for information about groups.

3 Complete these guidelines on conference organization using the definitions below to find the missing words. The first letter of each word is given to help you.
e.g. 1 = speakers'

A month before the conference, it is essential to request copies of the s___(1)___ papers and details of their timing. S___(2)___ requirements and the v___(3)___ must be confirmed, as must the contractor. The p___(4)___ and list of p___(5)___ must be ready for printing. Name b___(6)___, welcome banners, and vouchers must also be prepared. Official invitations must be sent to the p___(7)___ and any dignitaries. P___(8)___ leading the main s___(9)___ must decide on their chosen t___(10)___.

1 people making a speech or giving a talk
2 the total area allocated to the conference
3 place where the conference takes place
4 conference guide book
5 those taking part

6 identification labels
7 media
8 person who sits on the panel
9 items on the programme
10 subjects

Conference organizers must take seating layouts into careful consideration. Look at the arrangements below and decide which of the descriptions best suits them.

e.g. 1 = U-shape

classroom

discussion groups

theatre style

board of directors

hollow square

U-shape

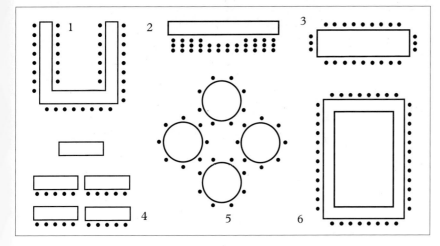

Follow-Up Activities

1 Describe a conference you have attended.

2 Do conferences vary significantly depending on the host country or are all international conferences more or less the same?

3 How important are the conference rooms and seating arrangements? What do you prefer and why?

4 Are conferences more important for their social value than for their content?

5 With the development of visual communications, will it be possible to participate in a conference without leaving the office?

Staff Motivation

A A good salary is not the only thing people look for in a job. The accompanying fringe benefits are also important. Identify the eight fringe benefits pictured here.

e.g. 1 = subsidized canteen

subsidized mortgage / relocation expenses / company car / interest-free loan on season ticket

subsidized canteen / medical insurance / discount on company goods / language training

B This article mentions a number of fringe benefits not pictured opposite. How many, and what are they?
e.g. expense account

The age of perks, packages and promises

An expense account with an extravagant entertainment allowance is the kind of perk which is now expected by company chairmen and chief executives. For middle managers, the company car is top of the league.

Despite government efforts to make these benefits less attractive, there is little evidence of any reduction in enthusiasm for them. Quite the opposite, in fact. The standard incentive package of a company car, a cheap mortgage and private healthcare is often now supplemented by a range of additional perks, designed to keep staff longer. These include longer holidays, relocation allowances and profit sharing. In addition, many firms are now offering child care facilities to encourage women back to work after raising their families.

A manager is describing the company he works for. What does he say about each of the following?

1 pay	2 training	3 work hours	4 management style	5 fringe benefits	6 job content
			e.g. *democratic*		

"Higgs Benson, a small printing business situated on the outskirts of Bradford, operates under the democratic leadership of Dwight Denby. Denby believes in delegating and in teamwork, so management is decentralized: from the most junior worker upwards, everyone has a say on how the business should be run.

Denby encourages his staff to attend day-release classes at the local college, so that they can improve their existing skills and acquire new ones. Salaries and wages are not above average, but perks include company cars, a good staff restaurant and free membership to a select sports club. Some of the staff work shifts, for example the print workers. Others are on flexitime, which means that they can plan their working day to suit their workload and their outside commitments. Everyone works a 35-hour week. Job rotation and job enrichment schemes are offered to people doing the more tedious jobs."

Follow-Up Activities

1 Describe the perks you have in your job.

2 Of the fringe benefits discussed in this unit, which three do you consider the most beneficial and why?

3 What are the areas of greatest - and least - job satisfaction in your company? What channels exist for improving work conditions?

4 Are perks simply a way for the employer to pay lower salaries?

5 Highly-motivated high-flyers tend to suffer from stress. Is this inevitable?

The European Market

Here are eight small businesses involved in the European Market. Match the people with their comments.

e.g. 6 = translator

Translator	Manufacturer	Publisher	Secretary

1 "We provide all the protective clothing for workers at our local airport. The trouble is a Spanish company has bid for the contract and we may lose it."

2 "We decided to open European offices to improve distribution of our encyclopaedias and reference works."

3 "I've been importing craft products from Hong Kong for six years. Now a Dutch colleague who helped me do some test marketing wants to take a franchise."

4 "I make water purifiers. I was doing well until I lost two contracts to a French competitor. We could have joined forces and then we would both have got the benefit."

5 "I have now joined a German legal practice, as I didn't think I would get enough European clients wanting to set up business in the U.K."

6 "I started a fax service by return to my clients. Now I've got so much work I have to give it to agencies."

7 "U.K. businesses who want to set themselves up at the Channel tunnel exit in France will need people like me. That's why my firm is buying its own development sites – so that we can get ahead of local construction firms."

8 "My London secretarial agency has got a branch in Paris and we are now beginning to make a good profit."

Retailer	Lawyer	Builder	Supplier

3 Read these ten questions.

1 How should I tackle the larger market?

2 How will European standards affect my product or service?

3 How can I be sure to cater for European tastes?

4 How do I protect my ideas and trademarks?

5 Do I need representation within the Economic Community?

6 Where do I get finance?

7 What are my business customers doing?

8 How do I stay ahead of the competition?

9 Will my employees need training?

10 Do I need a foreign partner?

Now choose the most appropriate suggestion for each question from this list.
e.g. 1 - *e*

a Banks have developed special finance packages.

b Carry out some market research when you are abroad at trade fairs.

c There may be benefits in setting up a joint venture.

d Try out your competitors' products yourself and seek advice from a consultancy firm.

e Watch out for opportunities when travelling abroad.

f Your business may need to improve sales techniques, export administration and management, as well as language skills.

g Talk to them and find out about their plans.

h You may need to consider wider protection, for example through the European Patent Office.

i Some products may have to be modified and feature dual language labelling.

j You will probably need the help of a reliable representative. Ask around existing contacts including suppliers.

List the fifteen words underlined above in the following categories.

e.g.
1 six business people: *customers,* _____ _____ _____

_____ _____

2 five professional/financial services: _____ _____ _____

_____ _____

3 four aspects of product development: _____ _____ _____

_____

Follow-Up Activities

1 What sort of language skills are needed for the single market? How can they be acquired?

2 What representation does your company have abroad? Do you consider it to be efficient and cost-effective?

3 In what ways could you re-design/adapt your products/ services to cater for a wider range of tastes and customs?

4 What state agencies are there in your country to help businesses export? Have you consulted any of them?

5 The single market should make business life in Europe much easier and create many more market opportunities . . . but will there also be losers?

Hotel Facilities

A The Majestic Hotel is a leading conference and banqueting venue that caters especially for a business clientele. Which of its facilities are represented by these twelve symbols below?

e.g. 1 = golf

Accommodation

800 bedrooms, of which 50 are luxury/VIP suites.

all prices inclusive of VAT and

* sumptuous buffet breakfast
* satellite TV & radio
* direct dial telephone
* hairdryer
* hospitality tray (tea/coffee/ chocolate/biscuits)
* complimentary newspapers
* bathroom
* telephone in executive rooms
* guest lounge
* room safe
* minibar
* international facsimile
* free parking

The Majestic has everything your company needs: 800 rooms including 50 suites, all with private bathroom, plus golf, tennis, a leisure complex with swimming pool, squash courts, gymnasium and sauna, full AV facilities available for hire, not to mention a helipad and a fleet of chauffeur-driven cars. Six new air-conditioned conference rooms, the largest accommodating 500 theatre-style, two exhibition halls, full secretarial services and, when the work's done, our own exclusive Crown Nightclub for relaxation.

Which of these facilities in the box on the left would you need to use if you wanted to:

13 leave your car?

14 lock up your passport and valuables?

15 call your head office quickly and privately?

16 invite some clients for informal discussion?

17 have a drink in your room?

18 send documents back to your colleagues?

Read this newspaper article and put the ten missing words back in the right places.

venues	over-pricing	packages	deluxe	chains
tariffs	stay	tailor-made	bar	suites

e.g. 1 = venues

Hotels: The Good News and the Bad News

Only one in five conference organizers feel hotels and other __(1)__ provide good value for money, according to a recent survey. Many of those questioned think that __(2)__ should vary according to the day of the week and the length of __(3)__. __(4)__ is a major problem, especially on audio-visual equipment, and delegates complain that they are often charged excessive __(5)__ prices.

As the conference business grows, many hotels are adding or expanding conference facilities. Large international hotel __(6)__ often now provide complete __(7)__ __(8)__ ,with full-time executive meeting planners who are responsible for all the organization and planning. Countryside settings are particularly popular with senior executives and may include __(9)__ accommodation with __(10)__ for VIP's.

Are the following statements true or false, according to the passage? Correct any false statements.

11 The majority of conference organizers are satisfied with their venues.

12 Hotel prices are cheaper mid-week.

13 Drinks in hotels are considered too expensive.

14 Senior executives prefer to be near international airports.

15 Hotels are not particularly interested in the conference business.

Match these inquiries and requests from hotel guests with the correct answer from the receptionist.   e.g. 1 = d

Guests

1 "I'd like a double room please."
2 "Could I have an alarm call tomorrow please?"
3 "Is breakfast extra?"
4 "I'd like to make a reservation for next week."
5 "What's the best way to get to the conference centre tomorrow?"
6 "I may be back rather late tonight and will need something to eat."

Receptionist

a "Complimentary limousine transportation is provided every morning."
b "Sorry, we're fully booked till the end of the month."
c "No, it's included in the nightly rate."
d "I'm afraid we only have singles available at the moment."
e "That's fine. We have 24-hour room service to suit all business schedules."
f "Certainly. What time?"

Follow-Up Activities

1 Describe the best and worst hotel you have ever stayed in.

2 When choosing a hotel, do you rely on guide books, travel agencies or personal recommendations? Are you normally satisfied with your choice?

3 What services and facilities do you consider most necessary for the business traveller?

4 Are international hotel standards consistent? Is the star system a reliable guide?

5 How do you see hotels developing in the future? (special hotels catering only for the business traveller/larger hotels/more exclusive hotels etc)

Bank Services

A Banks offer a wide range of services. Look at these eight customers and choose the leaflet that they each need.

e.g. 1 = credit + cash cards

Read this information about one bank's travel and holiday services.

When you travel . . .

Whether your journey is for holiday or business, we've the widest range of services to help you on your way.

Travellers Cheques
Available in most of the world's major currencies, these are both a safer way to carry cash – and in many countries the only legal way to travel with all you need. Our sterling travellers cheques are available over the counter in values of £10, £20, £50 and £100. They're accepted in hotels, restaurants and shops around the world and banks will cash them for a small charge.

Foreign Currency
We can meet all your requirements – and advise you of any local restrictions. Please try to order well in advance. Exchange rates fluctuate: a footnote on the application form explains how these are calculated. Before returning home, we suggest you spend any foreign coins locally, as these cannot be exchanged for sterling.

Eurocheques and Cards
Used like an ordinary cheque and guarantee card, these guarantee up to the equivalent of about £100 each, and can be used wherever you see the 'EC' symbol – at over 200,000 bank branches and five million retail outlets in 40 countries.

In most countries you write your Eurocheque in the local currency. When using or encashing more than two cheques at a time, you will be asked for identification – so it's a good idea to carry your passport with you.

Eurocheque books are issued free. The card itself is valid for up to two years, at a £5 annual fee.

Cardsafe
Register for Cardsafe protection for only £6 a year (£15 for three years) and safeguard all your credit and charge cards.

Are the following statements true or false according to the text? Give reasons.

	True	False	Explanation
1 Travellers cheques are cashed free of charge. e.g.		✘	*Banks will cash them for a small charge.*
2 Foreign currency does not always cost the same.			
3 Only foreign notes can be exchanged.			
4 Traveller's cheques must be presented with a guarantee card.			
5 You cannot use more than two Eurocheques to pay for any one purchase.			
6 You need a new Eurocheque card every two years.			
7 Each new Eurocheque card costs £5.			
8 If your traveller's cheques are stolen, you should contact Cardsafe for a refund.			

Match the word in list 1 with the correct word in list 2.

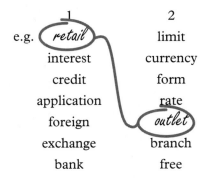

1	2
e.g. retail	limit
interest	currency
credit	form
application	rate
foreign	outlet
exchange	branch
bank	free

Follow-Up Activities

1 What services does your bank offer?

2 Describe in detail two bank services that you have used and found helpful.

3 Are banks becoming too powerful?

4 Which form of payment do you prefer to use abroad and why?

5 Will there be a world currency one day? Is the European ECU just the beginning? Would this standardization be in the interests of the banking system?

Retailing

The retailer is the manufacturers' link with the consumer. Here are sixteen vocabulary items connected with retailing. Use the ten underlined to label this picture of a sports outlet, and the remaining six to complete the sentences below.

logos	branded goods	closed circuit television	racks	shelf life	loss leader
own label goods	sales assistant	consumer durables		catalogue	margins
guarantee	bargain counter	point of sale		mark-up	display

e.g. 4 = own label goods

11 The manager decided to put the reduced cameras beside the entrance as a _____ _____ to encourage customers to come into the store.

12 One of the problems of selling fresh meat is that it has a short _____ _____.

13 A 15% _____ on all prices was needed to cover the increased production costs.

14 The market in _____ _____, such as dishwashers and refrigerators, is stagnant due to the recession.

15 In order to be competitive, the firm had to cut its profit _____ drastically.

16 Competitions with entry forms that consumers pick up at the _____ _____ _____ can be a very effective sales boost.

3 Retail outlets vary considerably in size, method of trading and location. Identify the eight types described below. All the words are in a box to help you.

e.g. 4 = shopping centre

1 _____ : all branches have the same name and are usually in town centres

2 _____ : have a shopping area larger than 50,000 square feet and are often on the outskirts of town

3 _____ : often move around to different sites, usually in the open air

4 _____ : the whole shopping area is closed to traffic

5 _____ : customers walk round with wire baskets or trolleys and help themselves

6 _____ : like to give personal attention to customers and often specialize in one type of product

7 _____ : stock a very wide range of goods and may have their own charge cards

8 _____ : customers buy from catalogues and receive goods by post

> stores
> shopping
> market
> stores
> order
> service
> mail
> independent
> market
> chain
> department
> stalls
> hyper-
> self
> centre
> shops

Wholesalers act as middlemen between manufacturers and retailers. They buy goods in bulk and sell them in smaller lots to the retail trade. But the increasing sophistication of modern retail distribution leaves little room for the wholesaler. Read this extract and put the five boxed words back in the right place.

e.g. 1 = Warehouses (and not premises)

The network of premises for the department store chain **Grapes** is one of the most advanced in Europe. Modern availability, transport stock, electronic links to all the stores, ensure an accurate reaction to sales, quicker distribution of warehouses and improved depots for customers.

Follow-Up Activities

1 What sort of retail outlets stock your company's products?

2 What sort of retail outlets do you prefer to use personally? Why?

3 What are the advantages and disadvantages of mail order?

4 Shopping by computer has been feasible for a number of years, but has not really taken off. Is shopping a basic human activity?

5 Goods may not always correspond to their descriptions. Should governments do more to protect consumers or is it a case of **caveat emptor** (let the buyer beware)?

Meetings

It has been estimated that eleven million meetings take place every day in the United States – so meetings must answer a real human need!

For a meeting to be effective, an agenda must be drawn up and circulated to all participants in advance. The agenda is a list of what will be discussed and follows a fixed order. The following five items appear on every agenda. Use the explanations to put them in their correct places.

next meeting / minutes of the previous meeting / AOB / apologies / matters arising

e.g. 1 = apologies

AGENDA

1 _____ (verbal or written and from those unable to attend)

2 _____ (notes from last meeting)

3 _____ (discussion about what has happened as a result of the last meeting)

4 _____ (anything else that participants wish to discuss)

5 _____ (time, date and place of the following meeting)

Minutes are normally taken by a secretary and signed by the chairperson to show that they are a correct record. Minutes can be long and almost word for word or they can be very brief, but they always include the following five facts. Complete the list by inserting the missing words.

e.g 6 = held

- The time and date of the meeting, where it was __(6)__ and who __(7)__ it.
- The names of all those __(8)__ and apologies for __(9)__ .
- All agenda items discussed and all __(10)__ reached.
- The time at which the meeting __(11)__ .
- The time, date and __(12)__ of the next meeting.

| decisions | place | held | present | chaired | absence | closed |

Read this extract from an article on the role of a chairperson.

The chairperson is in the driver's seat

A group of people meeting together can very often produce better ideas and decisions than a single person working alone. The original idea is challenged, tested and modified by argument and discussion until it is improved and sometimes transformed.

The chairperson's role is to guide, stimulate and summarize this debate - and stop it becoming heated and turning into a clash of personalities.

New and original suggestions are vital to the future development of any organization and must be encouraged, even if many of them will never actually be put into practice. It is all too easy for people to ridicule someone else's suggestion, especially if they are trying to enhance their own status. It is up to the chairperson to encourage members to turn suggestions into practical ideas.

Here are five nouns from the text. Give the corresponding verbs.

1 decision	decide
2 argument	
3 discussion	
4 suggestion	
5 development	

Here are five verbs from the text. Give the corresponding nouns.

6 modify	
7 improve	
8 transform	
9 summarize	
10 encourage	

Divide these eight items into two groups.

1 Methods of voting at meetings: e.g. postal

2 Occasions for people to meet together professionally

working party   postal   board meeting   show of hands

proxy   study group   secret ballot   AGM

Now find the six missing verbs to complete these sentences. The first letter is given each time to help you.   e.g. 3 = address

3 The chief accountant was invited to a_____ the meeting for ten minutes to explain the new pension scheme.

4 The marketing manager had to a_____ a shareholders' meeting all morning.

5 The chairwoman o_____ the meeting by thanking everyone for arriving so promptly.

6 As some vital documents had not been received, the meeting was p_____ until the following day.

7 Due to sickness, the meeting was c_____ and everyone was asked to submit their views in writing to the managing director instead.

8 An emergency meeting was c_____ for that afternoon to discuss the trade union's latest proposals.

Follow-Up Activities

1 What kind of meetings do you have to attend as part of your job? How frequent are they?

2 Describe the last meeting you went to. (agenda/decisions)

3 What is the optimum number of participants for a meeting and how long can a meeting usefully last?

4 Do you agree with the above article on the role of the chairperson? What else should a chairperson do?

5 Why are so many business meetings such a waste of time? How could this be avoided? (a phone call/a letter/a short conversation between individuals)

Cash and Currencies

Look at these two pictures and find the six objects in them which start
with the word **cash**.

e.g. cash sale

Here are eight more vocabulary items that include the word **cash**. Choose the correct definition.

e.g. 3 = *a*

3 to **cash a cheque** is to

a exchange a cheque for cash
b pay money into your account
c pay money into someone else's account

4 to **cash in** is to

a sell something (shares/traveller's cheques)
b pay cash for something (shares/traveller's cheques)
c open the cash register

5 to **cash in on** is to

a forecast the receipt of cash
b profit from something
c calculate money spent

6 a **cashier** is a

a dealer in foreign currency
b book in which payments are recorded
c person who pays and receives money

7 to **cash up** is to

a add up cash at the end of the day
b obtain cash from a bank
c get a reimbursement

8 a **cash crop** is

a the commission charged on foreign exchange
b something that is grown in order to be sold
c a company's reserves in cash for emergencies

9 **cash flow** is

a the conversion rate between currencies
b money which is immediately available
c the movement of money into and out of a business

10 **petty cash** is

a small denomination bank notes
b money held in a business to cover small expenses
c small denomination coins

Where do these currencies come from? The list of countries is given to help you.

1 peso *Mexico*	2 schilling	3 drachma	4 cruzado	5 krona	6 rupee	7 dollar
8 naira	9 zloty	10 lira	11 yen	12 pound	13 yuan	14 mark
15 rouble	16 escudo	17 shekel	18 baht	19 rial	20 dinar	21 peseta

Austria Brazil China Germany Greece India Iran Israel Italy Japan Mexico
Nigeria Poland Portugal Spain Sweden Thailand U.S.S.R. U.K. U.S.A. Yugoslavia

Read this newspaper article on Eastern Europe.

Cash is best when travelling in Eastern Europe

For travel in Eastern Europe, it is best to take cash in dollars, marks or pounds, though credit cards and traveller's cheques are good back-up and Eurocheques, too, can be useful.

In Hungary, the Soviet Union and Romania, according to regular visitors, the dollar is king, but the mark is preferred in Czechoslovakia. Pounds are accepted but not as popular.

In those countries with an active black market, taxi drivers will exchange money for you. They are normally reliable although they do not give top rates. Do not forget, however, that this is illegal. Traveller's cheques have one big disadvantage. Queues at banks and exchange bureaux can be so long that you may have to wait for several hours to get your money.

Now find:

e.g.
black market

1 three places to change money   _____ _____ _____

2 three currencies   _____ _____ _____

3 three countries that prefer dollars   _____ _____ _____

4 three other ways of paying   _____ _____ _____

Are these statements true or false, according to the article

5 The mark is more popular than the dollar in Romania.

6 The mark is more popular than the pound in Czechoslovakia.

7 Credit cards are not accepted in Eastern Europe.

8 It is illegal to exchange money with a taxi driver.

9 Taxi drivers give top rates of exchange.

10 You may have to wait a long time to cash traveller's cheques.

Follow-Up Activities

1 When do you use cash as a means of payment? (at home and abroad)

2 Are there occasions when you prefer to be paid in cash? Why?

3 Describe your country's currency in detail. (coins and notes of all denominations)

4 One problem with cash is that it is heavy. How could it be made lighter? (more notes/lighter metals/fewer small denominations)

5 Cash is certainly less used now than in the past. Will plastic money (cards) eventually take over completely?

Training

A Training is essential for any career in business and ranges from introductory and
general courses to extremely specialized intensive seminars for top executives.
Look at this programme for a course aimed at people who are planning to set up
their own business.

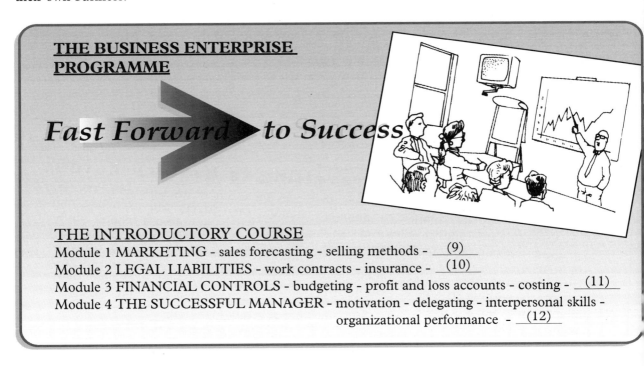

THE BUSINESS ENTERPRISE PROGRAMME

Fast Forward to Success

THE INTRODUCTORY COURSE
Module 1 MARKETING - sales forecasting - selling methods - ___(9)___
Module 2 LEGAL LIABILITIES - work contracts - insurance - ___(10)___
Module 3 FINANCIAL CONTROLS - budgeting - profit and loss accounts - costing - ___(11)___
Module 4 THE SUCCESSFUL MANAGER - motivation - delegating - interpersonal skills -
organizational performance - ___(12)___

Use the information in the programme to answer these questions about
course content.

Does the seminar include advice on how to:

	No	Yes	Details
1 estimate how much a project will cost?　e.g.		✗	*costing*
2 negotiate?			
3 balance the expenditure and income of a company?			
4 create publicity leaflets to send to potential clients?			
5 pass on authority to other team members?			
6 recruit staff?			
7 communicate effectively with staff and clients?			
8 predict sales figures accurately?			

Four components have been omitted from the course description. Insert them in
the correct modules.

cashflow　　　　　labour legislation　　　　　analysis and research　　　　　leadership

As well as giving money to people who are out of work (unemployment benefits), governments fund numerous training schemes (active labour-market measures). Look at the bar chart and read the text.

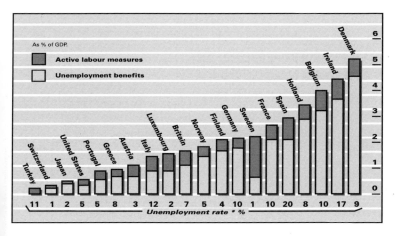

The governments of all the countries in the chart now support active unemployment measures such as training, but still spend much more on unemployment pay. The picture in Japan and the U.S. is not as black as it may appear, because much of their training is done privately. Differences in benefit spending perhaps reflect national character. The Danes appear keen to make their unemployed comfortable, whereas the Americans like to encourage jobhunting.

Find the answers to these six questions by looking at the bar chart.

e.g. 1 = Spain

1 Which country has the highest rate of unemployment?
2 Which country in the European Community has the lowest rate of unemployment?
3 Which country spends the highest percentage of GDP (Gross Domestic Product) on training schemes?
4 Which country spends the lowest percentage on training schemes?
5 Which country spends the highest percentage on unemployment benefits?
6 Which country pays no unemployment benefits?

Now read the text and say if these statements are true or false.

7 All the countries described spend some money on training.
8 The majority spend more on training than on unemployment benefits.
9 It is very difficult to get training in Japan or in America.
10 America pays low unemployment benefits to make people look for work.

Do you know the meaning of these words and expressions used in training?

1 Which is not a series of lessons designed to teach job skills?
   training course / training period / training programme

2 Which is not a person who is learning to do a job?
   trainee / training levy / apprentice

3 Which two are training at the place of work?
   training scheme / on-the-job training / in-house training

4 Which is an individualized training package?
   management training / cross-cultural training / tailor-made training

Follow-Up Activities

1 What training courses have you followed and how useful did you find them?

2 How is staff training organized at your place of work?

3 If you could have six months leave to follow a training course, what course would you choose and why?

4 Can training courses ever be as useful as practical on-the-spot work experience?

5 Is training a right? Many people are unable to follow training courses because their employers refuse to let them have time off for study and examinations. What measures could be taken to improve this situation?

Presentations

A

A speaker is going to address delegates at an international conference. All the special equipment and audio-visual aids have been prepared. Identify the ten items in the list.

e.g. 10 = Lectern

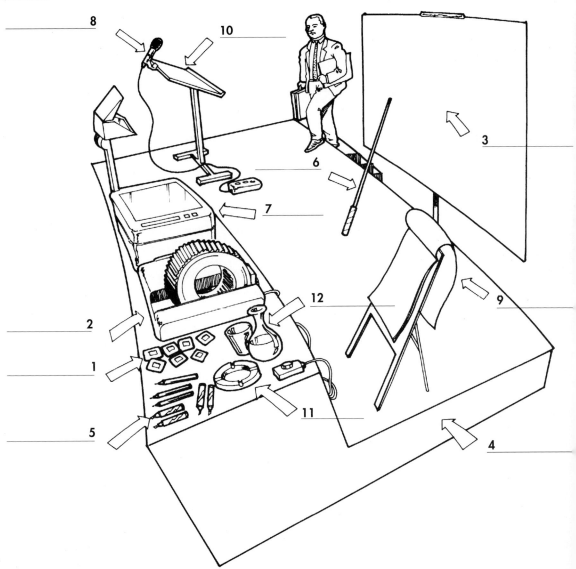

lectern	marker pens	flipcharts
overhead projector	pointer	slide projector
podium/platform	slides	
whiteboard/screen	microphone	

There are three other items on the table – small and yet important:

a glass, a (11) of water and an (12) .

Read these guidelines on choosing and organizing guest presenters
for a conference.

Guest speakers should always be experts in their profession and an eminent personality — not
necessarily in the profession — should always be chosen to open a conference by outlining its
theme. A call for papers from delegates attending the conference may lead to additional speakers.

If simultaneous interpretation is used, interpreters should receive a copy of all speeches well in
advance so they can familiarize themselves with the contents.

The organizer must brief speakers to make their speeches relevant to the topic and obtain an
abstract of the speech, plus a biography and picture of the speaker ahead of time (for use in the
programme, publicity material etc.).

Scan the text and find:
1 six people

e.g. guest speakers

2 six written items

Distinguish between the following pairs of words:

3 abstract/paper
Which is a short form of the other?

4 eminent/expert
Which is well-known and important?

5 theme/topic
Which is the main general idea?

Find words in the text that mean the following

6 giving a general description without many
details

7 extra

8 an immediate verbal translation of a speaker's
words

9 formal talk to an audience

10 give someone specific instructions

Many formal speeches begin in a similar way. Complete this
introduction. The first letter of each word is given to guide you.

e.g. 3 = pleasure

"Good evening l __(1)__ and g __(2)__ . As mayor, it is both a
p __(3)__ and a p __(4)__ to be invited to h __(5)__ this
international conference in this city and to be able to w __(6)__ so
many participants from all over the world. Speaking personally,
may I also say what an h __(7)__ it is to have been chosen to
o __(8)__ . . ."

Follow-Up Activities

1 Describe a presentation you
have made.

2 Do audio-visual aids make a
presentation more interesting
or do they distract from the
content of the speech?

3 What makes a good
presentation and a good
speaker? (content/style/voice/
manner)

4 Have you ever listened to
simultaneous interpreters?
How effective were they? Is
written translation better?

5 If you were organizing a
conference, who would you
choose as speakers and why?

Air Travel

A Heathrow Airport in London is the busiest international airport in the world, handling on average 100,000 passengers every day. Look at this extract from a passenger information leaflet and put the ten missing words back into their correct places.

take	declare	proceed	ending	follow
transfer	reclaim	fare	indicating	clear

e.g. 7 = take

ARRIVING AT LONDON AIRPORTS				TRANSPORT FROM HEATHROW TO CENTRAL LONDON	
Terminal arrivals	Follow the ARRIVALS sign if you are _(1)_ your journey in London or transferring to a UK Domestic flight.	**TRANSFERRING AT HEATHROW AIRPORT**		Transport into central London departs from the Arrivals Hall.	
	2 e.g. *d*	Transfer passengers	If you wish to _(9)_ to an International flight from Heathrow _(10)_ the TRANSFER signs.		Taxi Fare £19.00. Journey time 40 minutes.
Baggage Reclaim	From the Immigration Hall _(3)_ downstairs to _(4)_ your baggage from the carousel _(5)_ your flight number. Free trolleys are available for your bags.		11	⬤ Underground	Underground departs every 5 minutes. _(14)_ £2.10. Journey time 50 minutes.
Customs	To _(6)_ Customs _(7)_ the Red Channel if you have goods to declare or the Green Channel if you have no goods to _(8)_. You will then be in the Arrivals Hall.	 Transfer	12	 AIRBUS	Airbus to Victoria or Euston, departs every 20 minutes. Fare £5.00. Journey time 75 minutes.
			13	Heathrow-Reading Railair Link	15

Now insert these five missing texts to complete the information.

a
Railair coaches to Reading/ Woking are also available.

b
If you do not hold the above pass, follow the TRANSFER signs to the Transfer Desk where staff can help you.

c
Free transfer buses link all terminals. Simply follow the TRANSFER signs.

d
This will take you to the Immigration Hall where you must present your passport and any necessary visa/health documentation.

e
If you are holding this boarding pass, you have already been checked in for your next flight. Just follow the instructions on your pass and go directly to the departure terminal and gate

Complete this information about Heathrow's Terminal 4. There are twelve missing terms and a choice of three possibilities for each.
e.g. 1 = departure lounge

B.A.A. 4

Terminal 4

Terminal 4's most distinctive feature is its single ___(1)___ which measures 25 metres by 650 metres and replaces the conventional layout with separate aircraft ___(2)___ served by piers. The lounge contains a large ___(3)___ comprising several ___(4)___ areas and bars, numerous shops, including two ___(5)___ - free shops and a mobile ___(6)___ de change.

The departure hall houses 72 ___(7)___ desks, where baggage is ___(8)___ with a laser-readable bar code containing detailed information, including the bag's ___(9)___ and owner.

On arrival, passengers are helped through the terminal by ___(10)___ telling them where to find their ___(11)___ before they reach the reclaim hall and ___(12)___.

1   runway   departure lounge   flight indicator board

2   gates   tunnels   doors

3   quarantine station   moving walkway   shopping mall

4   police   catering   staff

5   duty   customs   security

6   desk   unit   bureau

7   control   handling   check-in

8   loaded   tagged   sorted

9   arrival   make   destination

10   trolleys   conveyor belts   monitors

11   baggage   flight   car park

12   VIP lounge   customs   taxis

How much do you know about air travel?

1 Try this quiz. Which countries do these well-known airlines come from?

Lufthansa   Pan Am   Aeroflot   Qantas

KLM   El Al   Olympic Airways   Iberia

2   Put two words together to make four doubles.

   jumbo   boarding   haul   number   jet   flight   long   pass

3   The aircraft landed on time. What is the opposite of **land**?

4   Is the longest runway at Heathrow 2.5 or 25 miles long?

5   Which channel do you go through if you have goods to declare to the customs?

Follow-Up Activities

1   Which airport do you know best? How do you rate its efficiency and its facilities?

2   How far do standards of service vary between the different airline operators? Which do you prefer?

3   Security is an ever-increasing problem. What else can be done to ensure the safety of air travellers and crew?

4   Air space is becoming more and more congested. What solutions are there to this problem?

5   How will air travel develop in the next century? Will most business companies have their own private aircraft?

Business-to-Business

Here are ten examples of the kind of advertisements which appear in the business-to-business section of a newspaper. Classify each one under the headlines given below.

Businesses for Sale

e.g.

1 *Businesses for Sale*

An established tool importer/distributor is for sale for genuine reasons. The company has an excellent range of products (with cable reel manufacturing facilities) which are sourced from wide-ranging international contacts.

Products are distributed nationally with some exports. T/O c. £750,000 with growth potential: serious enquiries only.

In the first instance telephone or <u>fax</u> for further details.

2

TO LET

HIGH QUALITY
BUSINESS
SPACE

15,000 to 40,000 sq ft and upwards units now nearing completion.
Virtually no external maintenance to buildings, no flat roofs.
Minimum tarmacadam paving since service areas are concrete paved and car park areas brick paved.
<u>Inquire</u> NOW for <u>Brochure</u> and Details.

3

SUPPLIERS OF NEW AND NEARLY NEW VEHICLES

Executive cars.........from £53.93 per week
Sports cars ....from £45.99 per week
Saloons ....from £29.96 per week
Commercials ....from £35.00 per week
Full <u>price list</u> available

4

COLOUR PHOTOCOPIER
with full edit facilities. 6 months old.
Only £700 + vat

5

YOUR U.S. OFFICE BASE

WASHINGTON D.C.
£30.00 Per week

- Full service office facility
- Phone number and business address
- Conference rooms and offices
- Personalized receptionist
- Fax, telex and word processing
- Form and service your U.S. Corporation and act as your registered agent
- Central prime downtown location convenient to Metro and airports

6

EXPERT BRITISH Computer Company with offices in the USA is willing to source hardware/software and also introduce British Products. We can promise reliability and a fast efficient service.

7

ENGLISH/ GERMAN.

Business + conference interpreting from £180 day.

8

LOANS
FOR ANY PURPOSE

Business or Personal
Secured or Unsecured
Fast and Friendly Service
Ring for a leaflet
FINANCIAL CONSULTANTS

9

ENVELOPES
AT LOW, LOW PRICES

DL	WHITE SHELF SEAL 4¼" x 8¾" Security Printed Interiors 1,000 @ £11.99 5,000 @ £11.29 per 1,000 10,000 @ £10.99 + VAT 50,000 @ £ 9.29	**DL**	WHITE GUMMED MAILING WALLET 4¼" x 8¾" 1,000 @ £10.99 5,000 @ £10.39 per 1,000 10,000 @ £ 9.99 + VAT 50,000 @ £ 8.59
C5	WHITE GUMMED MAILING WALLET 6¼" x 9" Security Printed Interiors 1,000 @ £16.60 5,000 @ £14.98 per 1,000 10,000 @ £13.89 + VAT 50,000 @ £11.98	**C5**	WHITE SELF SEAL MAILING WALLET 6¼" x 9" Security Printed Interiors 1,000 @ £18.99 5,000 @ £17.85 per 1,000 10,000 @ £16.29 + VAT 50,000 @ £14.49
C4	MANILLA GUMMED 12¾" x 9" 1,000 @ £25.89 5,000 @ £23.98 per 1,000 10,000 @ £22.98 + VAT 50,000 @ £19.88	**DL**	MANILLA GUMMED 4¼" x 8¾" 1,000 @ £7.95 5,000 @ £7.76 per 1,000 10,000 @ £7.29 + VAT 50,000 @ £6.89

<u>Send</u> for your free 24-page <u>catalogue</u>

10

SOLICITORS

**for Corporate Clients on Commercial Matters Throughout Europe including:
Mergers and Acquisitions
Joint Ventures
Commercial Contracts
International Banking
London Office:**

Leasing
Business services
Loans & finance
Office supplies

Translation
Legal services
Computers & computing services

Equipment
Commercial property
Businesses for sale

These six abbreviations are used in the advertisements. Write them out in full.

1 ¼′″   2 sq ft   3 c £750,000   4 @   5 T/O   6 per

e.g. 1 = a quarter of an inch (1 inch = 2.5 centimetres)

Now complete these two vocabulary networks using the eight underlined words in the advertisements.

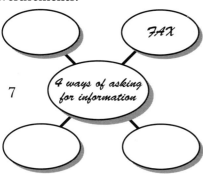

7 *4 ways of asking for information* — *FAX*

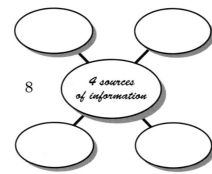

8 *4 sources of information*

Complete these two advertisements. Use the context to help you choose the right word from the list.

growth	**territory**	**automatically**	**accurate**
profitable	**record**	**trading**	**contractual**

BUSINESS SERVICES

BUSINESS RECORDING INTELLIGENCE KIT

- Credit Card Size Recorder, an exclusive miniature 4 hour recorder.
- Telerecorder (*no bigger than a cigarette pack*) will give you an ___(1)___ dependable ___(2)___ of all the calls that are made by taping them ___(3)___. Ensures no misunderstandings in important discussions, legal or ___(4)___.

Micro Hidden Bug Detector System lets you know if you're being bugged.

BUSINESS OPPORTUNITIES

UNIQUE PROVEN PRODUCT

£48K PLUS p.a. Opportunity right now!

Agents sought for highly ___(5)___ newventure. Can offer exclusive ___(6)___ and flexible ___(7)___ arrangements Our sales to businesses are booming and ___(8)___ accelerating. Respond early for our special low outlay offer.

Follow-Up Activities

1 Have you ever used this kind of business advertising? What for?

2 What are the advantages of business-to-business advertising in national newspapers?

3 Do you consider the Business Intelligence Kit to be a useful business aid? In what circumstances could it be used?

4 Is business-to-business advertising in newspapers the most effective way to reach potential clients? What other methods might be better?

NOTICE TO READERS
Whilst we take reasonable precautions with all advertisements, readers are strongly advised to take professional advice before paying a deposit or entering into any commitments.

5 Newspapers normally publish this kind of warning on the advertising pages. What risks make such a warning necessary? Is this type of warning sufficient?

Check you understand what these two terms mean. Choose the correct answer.

e.g. 1 = accurate

9 **bugged** means:
   a watched by hidden observers
   b secretly recorded by hidden microphones
   c photographed by hidden cameras

10 **outlay** means:
   a expenditure
   b tax restrictions
   c land for business premises

The Stock Market

Most free economies have stock markets to provide companies with a means of raising capital from investors in order to finance their businesses. How much do you know about the language of the stock market? Choose the right category for the words listed below.

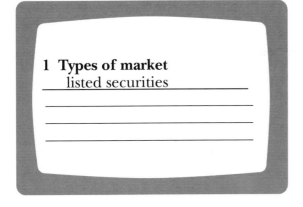

1 **Types of market**
   listed securities

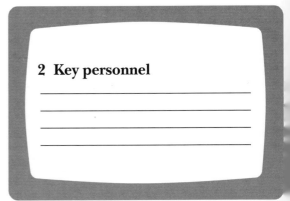

2 **Key personnel**

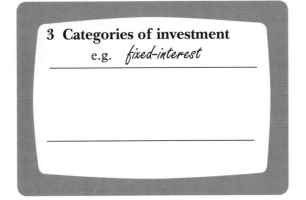

3 **Categories of investment**
   e.g. *fixed-interest*

4 **Types of stocks and shares**
   { _____ stocks
     _____ stocks
     _____ stocks
     _____ shares
   { _____ shares
     _____ shares

listed securities	loan	broker	preference
equities	domestic	unlisted securities	government
international	fund manager	analyst	fixed-interest
market maker	deferred	ordinary	debenture

Now match each of these terms with the correct definition below.

e.g. 1 = market maker

1 person or securities house which buys and sells shares for brokers on the Stock Exchange

2 investments where dividends are payable from profits remaining after fixed-interest charges

3 an agent who buys and sells shares for investors

4 Stock Exchanges like London, New York and Tokyo which deal in the stocks of multi-national companies

5 fixed-interest stocks, sometimes issued in a form that is convertible to ordinary shares at specified dates and prices

6   for companies which have obtained an official Stock Exchange quotation

7   investments where the rate of interest does not change

8   gilt-edged securities issued by the government to finance national requirements

9   for smaller companies not wishing to acquire a full Stock Exchange listing

10 person who examines different stocks and shares to evaluate their merits as investments

11 Stock Exchanges which deal mainly in their own country's shares

12 specialist responsible for funds entrusted to him for investment (e.g. unit trust, investment trust, pensions etc.)

The two animals opposite are also part of stock market language.

13 Which describes a person who sells stocks and shares anticipating a fall in the market price?

14 Which describes a person who buys stocks and shares anticipating a rise in the market price?

15 What do the expressions (a) **bear market** and (b) **bull market** mean?

Read this article and decide where these twelve words should go.

e.g 1 = blue-chip

blue-chip	listing	trading	unit trusts
bonds	investment	portfolio	valuation
dividend	flotation	offer	speculators

Easy access for investors

A highly specialized new telephone service claims to offer subscribers access to a complete range of up-to-date financial information at the touch of a button.

For investors in the most highly regarded industrial shares, there is news of __(1)__ prices. For those who have chosen to spread their __(2)__ over a variety of holdings, the bid and __(3)__ prices for all __(4)__ are listed in full. Others, who have put money in their local authority, can find out about their local __(5)__.

Investors who want to know what their __(6)__ is worth at any time can obtain an up-to-the-minute __(7)__. There are also details of companies seeking a full __(8)__ and of the __(9)__ of companies which are offering their shares for sale for the first time, not to mention __(10)__ results, __(11)__ payments and other important company announcements.

Something for everyone, including __(12)__ less interested in securing a steady income and possible capital appreciation than in making quick profits through market price fluctuations!

Follow-Up Activities

1   What is the status of your company?

2   Do you consider unit trusts to be a sound investment? If not, what would you recommend?

3   Would you find a subscription to an investment telephone service useful?

4   Is investing on the Stock Exchange by definition a risky business? Should there be more legislation to protect investors?

5   Is it inevitable that the stock market overheats from time to time?

Contracts

A

Here are some notes on an agreement between the Company of Professional Congress Organizers (C.P.C.O.), specialists in organizing congresses, and the Confederation of International Industries (C.I.I.), who are planning to hold a congress.

Contract Notes

Terms of agreement between C.P.C.O. and C.I.I. regarding The Industry Congress 1994:

C.P.C.O. shall

1 ___act___ as a consultant and make necessary arrangements for the conference.

2 _____ in planning meetings.

3 _____ the organizational and administrative work.

4 _____, immediately before and during the conference, a special office and secretariat.

C.I.I. shall

5 _____ responsible for the professional, technical and scientific content of the programme.

6 _____ a scientific secretariat.

C.P.C.O. agrees to

7 _____ a budget.

8 _____ fees.

9 _____ a final account of all receipts and expenditure.

C.I.I. agrees to

10 _____ an advance cash flow to the conference account until receipt of fees or other income.

11 _____ overall financial responsibility for the conference.

12 _____ C.P.C.O. to act on their behalf.

Cancellation: C.I.I. shall assume responsibility for all costs in the event of cancellation.

(Note: An appropriate arbitration clause with the title of an Arbitration Tribunal and the stipulation that any hearing be conducted in an acceptable language to both parties — should be included, along with details of the financial agreements already agreed.)

There are twelve verbs missing from the text. Choose the correct one from the three possibilities given below.

e.g.
1 (act) / present / be
2 participate / invest / address
3 require / undertake / meet
4 invite / set up / deliver
5 be / pay / earn
6 compete / provide / fax

7 purchase / trade / draw up
8 call / demonstrate / collect
9 sell / produce / let
10 count / maintain / solve
11 manufacture / accept / train
12 authorize / distribute / receive

What does the agreement say about these six questions, asked at a planning meeting. Complete the table.

	C.P.C.O.	C.I.I.	Not stated
e.g. 1		✗	
2			
3			
4			
5			
6			

There are fourteen words underlined in the text. Which eight match the definitions below?

1 an official meeting which is arranged to collect facts about a problem

e.g. *hearing*

2 person giving expert advice

3 settling of a dispute by an outside person

4 stopping of something planned from going ahead

5 section of a contract

6 a particular condition or requirement

7 the conditions of an agreement that must be accepted by both sides

8 companies or people involved in a legal agreement

Follow-Up Activities

1 What contracts have you signed or chosen not to sign?

2 Have you ever failed to fulfil a contract? Have you ever been let down by someone else? What happened?

3 Legal fees are a major cost in drawing up a contract. Are contracts really worth it for the protection and compensation they give?

4 What specific problems are involved in drawing up international agreements? (translation/legal systems)

5 Most contracts are very daunting, even for the well-informed. Should the language be simplified or would this lead to legal ambiguity?

Sponsorship

The organizer of the Banbury Golfing Championships is talking informally about the event's new sponsor, Keenan Sportswear. Choose one of the three possibilities given to fill in the missing words.

"We are delighted to have Keenan Sportswear ___(1)___ this year's Banbury Golfing Championships. They are now our ___(2)___ sponsor and, as such, they have ___(3)___ our ___(4)___ considerably. As you know, we have other sponsors, benefactors, and donors who are ___(5)___ us, but the association with a ___(6)___ company like Keenan Sportswear means a much bigger, ___(7)___ event altogether. With television ___(8)___ confirmed, there is no doubt that we are now the main event of the year. This is, of course, entirely compatible with Keenan Sportswear's ___(9)___ as an international leader in the field of sports clothing and equipment. And I am pleased to say that our re-designed ___(10)___ fully reflects the Banbury Golfing Championships' new status."

e.g. 1 attending / <u>sponsoring</u> / briefing

    2 donor / in kind / prime

    3 launched / boosted / appointed

    4 capital funding / advertising agency / sales forecast

    5 plugging / auditing / supporting

    6 potential / prestigious / principal

    7 high class / lower profile / higher profile

    8 channel / feedback / coverage

    9 identification / image / feature

    10 logo / brand / label

3 Match each comment on the left with an appropriate response from the right

e.g. 1 = b

1 "In Britain nearly £35 million a year go to sponsoring the arts."	a "People who go the theatre or are on theatre mailing lists tend to be the wealthy members of society."
2 "I've heard that firms have invited executives from the theatres they sponsor to attend in-house training schemes."	b "And that figure is expected to double by 1995."
3 "Surely sponsorship is restricted to giant multi-nationals."	c "The idea is to help artistic directors learn management skills."
4 "What sort of target audience does arts sponsorship reach?"	d "Yes, like any business expense."
5 "Why would an insurance company sponsor a rock concert?"	e "No, many small and medium-sized firms sponsor projects, often at a regional level."
6 "Is money spent on sponsorship tax-deductible?"	f "To change their image and appear more modern so they can appeal to younger policyholders."

Choose a word from list 1 and a word from list 2 to make four doubles.

	1	2
e.g.	business	audience
	tax	expense
	multi-	company
	mailing	lists
	target	deductible
	insurance	nationals

Follow-Up Activities

1 Have you attended any sponsored events or performances? Do you think it was a good form of promotion?

2 What sort of public events has your company sponsored? What might it sponsor in future?

3 What are the risks in sponsorship? Can they be minimized?

4 Do you think sponsorship is a growth area? What other events and occasions could be sponsored and how?

5 Is there a danger of sponsors having too much power, for example over the choice of programme or seat allocation?

Terms of Employment

Eight candidates interviewed for a job all had concerns about the company's employment terms and conditions. Which point in its contract summary answers their questions?

e.g. 5 = *a*

The appointment will be subject to the following terms and conditions:

a Hours of work: flexitime in operation. Some week-end work. Time off will be given in lieu. Annual leave: 30 days plus public holidays.

b Sickness leave: during the first year of employment, one quarter of the working year at full pay, rising by stages to a full working year at full pay after six years' services. Free medical insurance after two years' service.

c Maternity leave: entitlement additional to the statutory requirements, subject to two years' service.

d Family leave: staff are entitled to seven days' leave at full pay, followed by seven days' unpaid leave per annum in the case of urgent family commitments.

e Salary will be on the senior management scale with performance-related increments and annual bonus scheme.

f Pension: all staff must join the pension scheme. The present level of contribution is: employee 6%, employer 17%. A death in service benifit of three times annual salary is payable for all permaneny staff. Retirement age for all employees is 65.

g Trade union: staff have the right to belong to a trade union, but membership is not obligatory.

h Notice: three months' written notice is required on either side.

I plan to start a family fairly soon and may need six months off after the birth.

1

My father is due to have a serious operation at the end of the year. What's the position if I need time off to visit him?

2

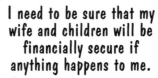

I'm non–political and do not wish to join any workers organisation.

3

I need to be sure that my wife and children will be financially secure if anything happens to me.

4

If I have to work on a Saturday will I be paid overtime?

5

Will the standard of my work be reflected in my salary?

6

Presumably I can make my own pension arrangements, I already have a private plan.

7

If I decide to terminate our contract, can I leave immediately?

8

3 Use the information in this bar chart to find the three countries and two nationalities that are missing from the text.

e.g. 1 = Dutch

The average ___(1)___ worker only clocks up 34 hours a week compared with his ___(2)___ counterpart who works 47 hours. One reason for such a big difference is the number of workers who are part-time: one in four of Holland's workforce is part-time, more than twice the number in Japan. Holidays reflect differences too: five weeks in Holland while the Japanese are only entitled to 15 days, and many take less. In most OECD countries the official working week was trimmed during the 1980s and paid holidays were lengthened. However, in ___(3)___, hours worked were unchanged and in two countries, ___(4)___ and ___(5)___, they actually increased over the decade.

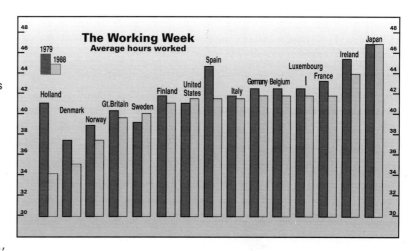

The Working Week
Average hours worked

1979 1988

Holland, Denmark, Norway, Gt.Britain, Sweden, Finland, United States, Spain, Italy, Germany, Belgium, Luxembourg, France, Ireland, Japan

Check you know the meaning of these words in the text. Choose the word or expression that is closest in meaning.

6 **clocks up**
a works overtime for
b reaches a total of
c does not count the time spent for

7 **workforce**
a manual workers who are not in management
b those of working age (18-65)
c all the workers in a particular company, area or country

8 **counterpart**
a workmate
b employee
c equivalent

9 **are entitled to**
a are limited to
b have a right to
c are required to take

10 **trimmed**
a reduced
b legalized
c abolished

Follow-Up Activities

1 How many hours do you work? Does it vary from week to week?

2 What is your holiday entitlement and how does it compare with the national average?

3 Do the figures in the bar chart above surprise you? Do some nations really work harder than others?

4 What are the advantages and disadvantages of flexitime?

5 Should there be more legislation to protect workers in your country? How would this affect unemployment?

Patents

Applying for a patent is a long, complicated and expensive process, usually best undertaken by a patent agent. Look at this flowchart and note the specialized vocabulary. There are twelve spaces in the text. First try to work out what sort of words are missing, then choose from the list below to complete the summary.

e.g. 1 = abstract

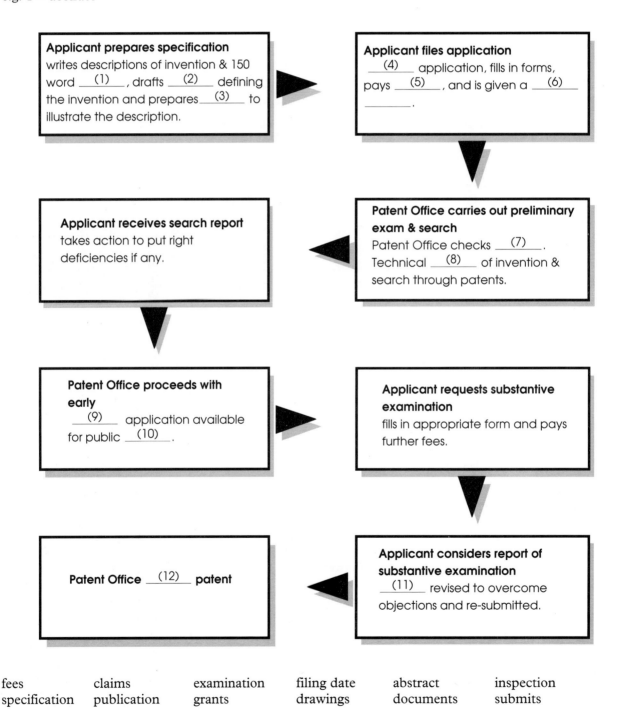

Applicant prepares specification
writes descriptions of invention & 150 word __(1)__, drafts __(2)__ defining the invention and prepares __(3)__ to illustrate the description.

Applicant files application
__(4)__ application, fills in forms, pays __(5)__, and is given a __(6)__ _____.

Patent Office carries out preliminary exam & search
Patent Office checks __(7)__.
Technical __(8)__ of invention & search through patents.

Applicant receives search report
takes action to put right deficiencies if any.

Patent Office proceeds with early
__(9)__ application available for public __(10)__.

Applicant requests substantive examination
fills in appropriate form and pays further fees.

Patent Office __(12)__ patent

Applicant considers report of substantive examination
__(11)__ revised to overcome objections and re-submitted.

fees	claims	examination	filing date	abstract	inspection
specification	publication	grants	drawings	documents	submits

3 Read this short article. Once again twelve words are missing. This time choose the correct one from the three possibilities given below.

TAKING OUT A PATENT TODAY

The patenting of new __(1)__ has two objectives: one is to provide an __(2)__ to inventors by granting them a temporary __(3)__ on the __(4)__ of their invention. The other objective is to __(5)__ and facilitate __(6)__ progress and __(7)__ by assuring the publication of new inventions. However, it can take more than four years before a patent is granted and there is a huge __(8)__ of applicants. This delay is difficult for a small business or an individual inventor who depends on the __(9)__ of his patent for its exploitation. __(10)__ actions can be brought only after the patent has been granted and do not offer any real __(11)__ against a financially strong competitor who can afford the cost of patent __(12)__.

---

e.g. 1 activities / inventions / sales

2 incentive / example / outline

3 registration / assistance / monopoly

4 exploitation / development / analysis

5 adjudicate / produce / stimulate

6 technological / fiscal / theoretical

7 policies / innovation / ratification

8 increase / input / backlog

9 cover / licensing / classification

10 representation / marketing / infringement

11 protection / issue / legislation

12 consultation / procedure / litigation

Here are four questions and answers about intellectual property rights — but the words in the questions have been mixed up. Read each answer first to give you an idea of the question, then put the words into the correct order.

1 Can / be / without / an / patent / invention / exploited / a?
   Yes, providing no-one else already has rights protecting that invention.

2 apply / of / Does / to / copyright / authors / only / work / the?
   No, it also covers musical and artistic work, for example.

3 design / a / always / Is / trademark / a?
   A brand name can also be registered.

4 when / patent / does / What / it / is / mean / pending / a?
   It means that the invention has been put on the market before a patent has been granted.

Follow-Up Activities

1 Does your company hold any patents? Have you ever had an idea that you considered patenting?

2 How would you advise somebody to exploit an innovation? Patent it and then exploit it himself? Sell the idea to a big company? Engage in some kind of co-operative project?

3 What are the advantages and disadvantages of issuing patents for a limited period of time?

4 Many inventors are discouraged by the time, money and effort involved in patent application and never exploit their ideas. Could the whole process be simplified?

5 Patent litigation is beyond the means of the average individual or small company. What does this mean in practice?

Business News

Every day the world's newspapers and specialist magazines publish a huge amount of business information with facts, figures and comments. Read these short articles quickly to get an idea of the subjects they cover. Then match each text with one of these topics.

environment-friendly products	job losses	joint venture
merger	legal action	market trends
labour dispute	new appointment	

e.g. 1 = merger

1

Conways and Italy's **Multifibre** are to merge their acrylic fibre businesses in Spain.

2

Williams Petroleum Incorporated and Lychizawa Chemicals are to consider the joint manufacture of diphenyl methane diisocyanate at a location to be decided in Western Europe.

3

TWO candidates are being considered to take over as chief executive at Hodfield's, the clothing and furniture retailer, in place of Peter Grime who resigned a week ago.

4

West European new car sales remain flat. The total in the first seven months of this year was down 0.3 % on the same period last year.

5

A court bid to end a three–week sit–in by workers was adjourned today. After hearing that both sides needed more time to prepare the case, Lord Gilgan adjourned the case until Thursday.

6

BEING GREEN CAN PAY!
Frigozone will get $180 m from Russia for supplying the know–how to build ozone–friendlier fridges.

7

Davies and Smart, one of the Pentagon's top defence contractors will cut 14,000–17,000 jobs this year. The plan is to trim the company's expenses by $700m annually.

8

America's songwriters and music publishers want a New York federal court to stop manufacturers selling digital audio tape recorders and blank cassettes in America, to curb home taping of copyright material

These sentences are the continuation of four of the newsbriefs opposite. Match each one with the correct article.

10   Only two western car makers have improved their performance.

12   The deal may lead to other projects for the company.

The plant will cost about £200 million.

11

9   One is believed to be currently Chief Executive of a competitor.

Find the words in the articles which match these definitions
(the number in brackets shows you which article you look at).

e.g. 1 = location

1	site (2)	6	postponed (5)
2	most important (3)	7	knowledge (6)
3	gave up his job (3)	8	leading (7)
4	low (4)	9	cut (7)
5	protest (5)	10	reduce (8)

All the words and phrases in this short news item have been mixed up.
Put them back in the correct order.

CHEWING GUM CAN BE DANGEROUS FOR YOUR HEALTH!

The watchdog		has said
		because it contains
		other foodstuffs.
		Food Commission
		chewing gum
		mineral hydrocarbons
		a health warning on the packet
		banned from
		should carry
		The watchdog

What products carry health warnings on the packet in your country?

Follow-Up Activities

1 Which publications do you read in English? What sort of articles do you find interesting?

2 Choose two business articles from your own reading to summarize in your own words.

3 Write a sentence to continue the other four articles on the previous page.

4 What do you think are the best international business publications on sale at the moment? Why?

5 How much power does the press have over the business world?

Franchising

There are 300 franchisors in Britain servicing more than 16,000 franchised outlets with total sales of £5 billion. A breakdown of this turnover by sector is shown in these pie charts.

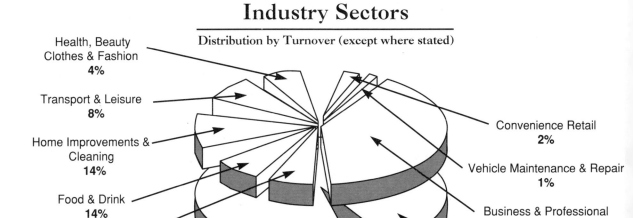

Industry Sectors

Distribution by Turnover (except where stated)

Health, Beauty Clothes & Fashion 4%

Transport & Leisure 8%

Home Improvements & Cleaning 14%

Food & Drink 14%

Print 15%

Property Based 56% (Units)

Business-to-Business 45%

Convenience Retail 2%

Vehicle Maintenance & Repair 1%

Business & Professional Services 42%

Mobile / Home Operators 44% (Units)

Retail Sales 55%

Where do these eight business operations fit into the top pie chart

e.g. 1 = food & drink

1 restaurants and fast-food outlets

2 fast print centres, artwork & design, commercial copying

3 interior decorating

4 overnight parcels collection & delivery

5 24-hour mini-markets

6 retailing of ladies' and men's fashion

7 employment agencies

8 commercial vehicle car-washes

Place these three businesses on the middle pie chart.

9 health juice bar

10 car engine tuning at customers' homes

11 door-to-door handcleaning of carpets and upholstery

Now look at the bottom pie chart and distinguish between those that serve the general public and those that serve other businesses.

12 suppliers of ceramic tiles to the trade

13 garden maintenance of commercial and industrial sites

14 super-saver store for cut-price household goods

3 Read this article about franchising. There are ten words missing. Look at the three possibilities given below and choose the correct one for the context.

Live happily ever after with a franchise

Franchising has caught the imagination of many would-be ___(1)___ as a way of ___(2)___ their own business and people from all ___(3)___ have joined the franchise system in recent years. Taking on a franchise with one of the more ___(4)___ and well-established operations and raising finance through a ___(5)___ bank usually reduces the ___(6)___ risk — neither the banks nor the established ___(7)___ want the ___(8)___ to fail, so their ___(9)___ procedures to eliminate those who are ___(10)___ are very strict and thorough.

1 personnel / entrepreneurs / staff

2 running / doing / working

3 branches / backgrounds / training

4 large / specialized / reputable

5 clearing / central / federal

6 big / first / potential

7 outlet / franchisor / institution

8 franchisee / applicant / membership

9 financial / screening / education

10 independent / motivated / unsuitable

These eight words and phrases are often used in connection with franchising. Five are the responsibility of the franchisor, three of the franchisee. Which is which?

tight controls   national advertising
company back-up   overheads
ongoing training   quality specifications
working capital   lease premium

1 franchisee

2 franchisor

e.g. *tight controls*

Follow-Up Activities

1 Give some examples of franchises in your country. Are they doing well?

2 If you took out a franchise, what sort of product or service would you choose? Why?

3 Although franchising reduces the risk in a new business venture, it does not guarantee success. Why do you think a percentage of franchisees still fail?

4 Franchising increases uniformity. Is restricted consumer choice the price for quality guarantees?

5 Is franchising a kind of monopoly and therefore contrary to the spirit of free competition? Should it be banned?

Answers

Statistics

A 1 turnover remained constant   2 profits declined sharply   3 sales fell gradually 4 costs reached a peak   5 demand rose sharply   6 overheads levelled off   7 prices fluctuated   8 output increased gradually

B 1 climbed, rose, increased, grew 2 interest, payments, mortgage, prices 3 last, past, seasonal, previous   4 statistics 5 income

C 1 bar chart   2 pie chart

Import/Export

A 1 standard shipping note d   2 customs declaration form b   3 letter of credit c 4 packing list f   5 air waybill h 6 certificate of origin g   7 certificate of insurance a   8 bill of lading e

B 1 f   2 a   3 d   4 g   5 e   6 c   7 i   8 j 9 h   10 b

C f.a.s.-free alongside ship, c.i.f.-cost, insurance, freight, c. and f-cost and freight, f.o.b.-free on board.1 a, b   2 a, b, c, d 3 a, b, c, d, e   4 a, b, c

Insurance

A 1 legal expenses   2 goods in transit 3 burglary and theft   4 public liability 5 cost of replacing glass in shop windows 6 theft of money from premises   7 cost of compiling computer records again if damaged   8 business interruption or consequential loss   9 damage to stock 10 product liability   11 employer's liability 12 cost of changing locks following theft of keys

B 1 branches   2 premium   3 cover 4 comprehensive   5 policyholders 6 discounts   7 rates   8 claims   9 broking 10 underwriting   11 risk   12 loss

C 1 actuary   2 assessor   3 agent   4 adjuster

Telephoning

A 1 pay phone   2 car phone   3 mobile phone   4 answer phone   5 memory 6 handset   7 switchboard   8 operator 9 directory   10 phone card

B 1 false (0.2% in the U.K. and 1% in Sweden)   2 true   3 false (France is five times as expensive as the U.K.)   4 true 5 a   6 a   7 c   8 c

C 1 Could I speak to   2 extension   3 Hold on   4 put you through   5 line   6 engaged 7 leave a message   8 call me back

Computers

A 1 word processor   2 modem   3 personal computer   4 screen   5 keyboard 6 printer   7 monitor   8 mouse 9 portable computer   10 external single disk drive

B 1 high-resolution   2 high-level 3 upgradable   4 compact   5 compatible 6 laser   7 single   8 3˘"   9 non-glare 10 dot matrix
Michael Riccioli chose the computer.

C microprocessor   spreadsheet   floppy disk printout   laptop   network

Recruitment

A 1 a   2 d   3 f   4 c   5 e   6 b

B 1 liaison with speakers, preparing publicity material, develop existing contacts, co-ordination of technical support staff   2 eye for detail, sense of humour, self-starter, highly motivated   3 MBA, good organizational skills, PC experience, ability to negotiate   4 potential for rapid promotion, profit sharing, relocation assistance, assistance to study

C 1 ambitious   2 record   3 maximum 4 communicator   5 knowledge 6 competitive   7 bonus   8 benefits

Company Structure

A 1 sales & marketing   2 production
3 administration   4 legal   5 transport
6 R & D   7 personnel   8 accounts
9 personnel   10 administration   11 legal
12 transport   13 sales & marketing
14 administration   15 R & D
16 accounts   17 sales & marketing
18 personnel   19 purchasing
20 production

B 1 involvement   2 growth   3 face-to-face
4 labour   5 scales   6 decision-making
7 in-house   8 policies   9 reviews
10 notice   11 regular   12 representatives

C 1 sole trader   2 partnership   3 private
limited company   4 public limited
company

Bank Forms

A 1 d   2 c   3 b   4 a   5 f   6 e

B 1 Title   2 block capitals   3 Postcode
4 tick   5 monthly statement   6 Financial
7 Bank Sort Code   8 Deposit   9 Nature
of Business   10 income   11 Position
12 self-employed   13 accountant   14 sign
15 check

Correspondence

A 1 f   2 h   3 k   4 g   5 i   6 e   7 b   8 l
9 j   10 d   11 c   12 a

B 1 false (if you know the name you should
always use it)   2 false (**Ms** is used for both
married and unmarried women – there is no
plural form)   3 false (**Mister** is not correct
and should not be used)   4 true (there are
some differences in style between British
and American letters)   5 true (this is to
encourage custom)   6 false (**Inc.** –
Incorporated – is used in the U.S.A.)
7 true (Americans usually put the month
before the day e.g. 2.10.90 means
10 February not 2 October 1990)   8 false
(it will close **Yours faithfully**)   9 true
(it's an abbreviation for the Latin **per
procurationem**)   10 false (it provides
proof of delivery, but for compensation the
registered mail service must be used)

C 1 dictated   2 typed   3 signed   4 folded
5 sealed   6 addressed   7 stamped
8 posted

Marketing

A 1 product   2 price   3 promotion   4 place
5 research   6 development   7 strategy
8 costing   9 distribution   10 consumer

B 1 "packaging as a means to lure shoppers"
2 "toiletries are not quickly thrown away so
their design may be more stylish than, say,
baked beans which are kept in a cupboard"
3 "protecting the product"   4 "it can
promote the quality of a product"   5 "one
basic design principles, though: it should
stand out on the shop shelves"
6 re-designed   7 contents   8 graphics

C 1 Lancashire   2 Griffin's   3 7 ³/₈oz (ounces)
4 73p (pence)   5 0 317600 083078   6 keep
refrigerated   7 until 25th September   8 £1.58
per lb (pound)

Transport

A 1 c   2 f   3 e   4 a   5 d   6 b   7 weighed
8 packed   9 retail outlets   10 docked   11 port
12 containers   13 hold   14 cartons
15 distribution   16 quality control   17 random
check   18 lorries

B 1 door-to-door service, not tied to any timetable,
no need for transhipment, can reach places
inaccessible to other forms of transport   2 good
for bulk commodities in large quantities, most
economical on fuel, especially suitable for
containers   3 reduced insurance costs due to
shorter transit time, fastest over long distances
4 delayed by traffic congestion in cities   5 routes
limited by lines and stations   6 weight and size of
cargo limited, high freight rates

C 1 road   2 air   3 road   4 rail   5 rail   6 road

Business Mail

A 1 chairman's statement   2 registration form
3 periodical   4 admission card   5 invoice
6 subscription offer   7 price list   8 report
9 statement of account   10 mail shot

B 1 2, 4, 5, 6, 10   2 2, 5, 6   3 1, 3, 7, 8, 9
4 5, 9

C 1 Belgian francs   2 value added tax   3 number
   4 at   5 per annum   6 percent   7 post office
   8 quarter   9 forward   10 March   11 April
   12 United States

Career Profiles

A 1 e   2 o   3 a   4 k   5 n   6 p   7 g, h, m   8 d
   9 c   10 l   11 b, f, i   12 j

B 1 awards   2 competition   3 competitors
   4 expand   5 operations   6 fare   7 buy up
   8 dividend   9 genius   10 highlight

C 1 a (retail experience)   2 b (in Spain, Europe or
   Latin America)   3 c (own business)
   4 c (specializing in property)   5 b (hands on)
   6 b (£5/20 million)   7 c (miss this opportunity at
   your peril!)   8 a (performance related)

Fax

A 1 10 sheet automatic document feeder   2 up to
   A4 width scanning   3 dialling keys   4 16 digit
   liquid crystal display   5 facsimile

B 1 c   2 g   3 a   4 d   5 h   6 e   7 f   8 b

C 1 e   2 d   3 b   4 a   5 c

Bank Cards

A 1 e   2 b   3 h   4 d   5 a   6 f   7 g   8 c   9 M.
   Stephens   10 £49.93   11 28.09.91   12 The
   Clothing Store

B 1 g, i, j   2 b, d, l   3 c, e, k   4 a, f, h

C 1 payment cards   2 6   3 the bank

Advertising

A 1 jingles   2 competitions   3 gimmicks
   4 introductory offers   5 money-off coupons
   6 window display   7 free samples
   8 demonstrators

B 1 television (commercials)   2 national press
   3 (commercial) radio   4 (consumer) magazines
   5 hoardings (posters)

C 1 appeal   2 launch   3 attract   4 project
   5 boost   6 spend   7 persuade   8 promote

Car Hire

A 1 c   2 a   3 d   4 a   5 c   6 d   7 b   8 d   9 a
   10 c

B 1 no (I was kept waiting for 20 minutes)   2 yes
   (an impressive-looking car)   3 yes (the smooth
   ride)   4 no (ashtray already full of ash)   5 no
   (offered neither explanation nor refund)   6 no (I
   had no idea how to use many of them)   7 no
   (when I finally managed to find your office)
   8 no (computer was out of order)

Conferences

A 1 d   2 f   3 g   4 e   5 b   6 c   7 a   8 h

B 1 speakers'   2 space   3 venue   4 programme
   5 participants   6 badges   7 press   8 panellists
   9 sessions   10 topics

C 1 U-shape   2 theatre style   3 board of directors
   4 classroom   5 discussion groups   6 hollow
   square

Staff Motivation

A 1 subsidized canteen 2 company car   3 discount
   on company goods   4 medical insurance
   5 subsidized mortgage   6 relocation expenses
   7 language training   8 interest-free loan on
   season ticket

B Five additional fringe benefits are mentioned:
   expense account, entertainment allowance, longer
   holidays, profit sharing, child care facilities

C 1 not above average   2 day-release classes
   encouraged   3 either shift work or flexitime,
   35-hour week   4 democratic, delegation,
   teamwork, decentralized   5 company cars, staff
   restaurant, free sports club membership   6 job
   rotation and job enrichment schemes in place

The European Market

A 1 supplier   2 publisher   3 retailer
   4 manufacturer   5 lawyer   6 translator
   7 builder   8 secretary

B 1 e   2 i   3 b   4 h   5 j   6 a   7 g   8 d   9 f
   10 c

C   1 customers, partner, competitors, representative, contacts, suppliers   2 finance packages, market research, consultancy, export administration, management   3 standards, trademarks, patent, labelling

Hotel Facilities

A   1 golf   2 squash courts   3 audio-visual facilities   4 gymnasium   5 large conference room   6 nightclub   7 secretarial services   8 tennis   9 a leisure complex with swimming pool   10 sauna   11 helipad   12 chauffeur-driven cars   13 free parking   14 room safe   15 direct dial telephone   16 guest lounge   17 minibar   18 international facsimile

B   1 venues   2 tariffs   3 stay   4 over-pricing   5 bar   6 chains   7 tailor-made   8 packages   9 deluxe   10 suites   11 false (only about 20% are satisfied)   12 false (people think they should vary)   13 true (hotel bar prices are described as excessive)   14 false (many like countryside settings)   15 false (they are increasing their conference facilities)

C   1 d   2 f   3 c   4 b   5 a   6 e

Bank Services

A   1 credit and cash cards   2 personal loans   3 standing orders   4 foreign currency   5 personal pensions   6 executor services   7 high-interest deposit accounts   8 overdraft facilities

B   1 false (banks will cash them for a small charge)   2 true (exchange rates fluctuate)   3 true (foreign coins cannot be exchanged)   4 false (it's Eurocheques that need a guarantee card)   5 false (you can encash more than two with identification)   6 true (each Eurocheque card is valid for up to two years)   7 false (£5 has to be paid every year)   8 false (it only protects credit and charge cards)

C   retail outlet, interest-free, credit limit, application form, foreign currency, exchange rate, bank branch

Retailing

A   1 logos   2 branded goods   3 catalogue   4 own label goods   5 sales assistant   6 racks   7 guarantee   8 bargain counter   9 display   10 closed circuit television   11 loss leader   12 shelf life   13 mark-up   14 consumer durables   15 margins   16 point of sale

B   1 chain stores   2 hypermarket   3 market stalls   4 shopping centre   5 self-service   6 independent shops   7 department stores   8 mail order

C   1 warehouses   2 premises   3 depots   4 stock   5 availability

Meetings

A   1 apologies   2 minutes of previous meeting   3 matters arising   4 A.O.B. (any other business)   5 next meeting   6 held   7 chaired   8 present   9 absence   10 decisions   11 closed   12 place

B   1 decide   2 argue   3 discuss   4 suggest   5 develop   6 modification   7 improvement   8 transformation   9 summary   10 encouragement

C   1 postal, show of hands, proxy, secret ballot   2 working party, board meeting, AGM, study group   3 address   4 attend   5 opened   6 postponed   7 cancelled   8 called

Cash and Currencies

A   1 cash dispenser, cash card   2 cash box, cash sale (purchase), cash register, cash desk   3 a   4 a   5 b   6 c   7 a   8 b   9 c   10 b

B   1 Mexico   2 Austria   3 Greece   4 Brazil   5 Sweden   6 India   7 U.S.A.   8 Nigeria   9 Poland   10 Italy   11 Japan   12 U.K.   13 China   14 Germany   15 U.S.S.R.   16 Portugal   17 Israel   18 Thailand   19 Iran   20 Yugoslavia   21 Spain

C   1 black market, banks, exchange bureaux   2 dollars, marks, pounds   3 Hungary,

Soviet Union, Romania   4 credit cards, traveller's cheques, Eurocheques   5 false   6 true   7 false   8 true   9 false   10 true

Training

A   1 yes (costing)   2 no   3 yes (profit and loss accounts)   4 no   5 yes (delegating)   6 no   7 yes (interpersonal skills)   8 yes (sales forecasting)   9 analysis and research   10 labour legislation   11 cash flow   12 leadership

B   1 Spain   2 Luxembourg   3 Sweden   4 Japan   5 Denmark   6 Turkey   7 true   8 false   9 false   10 true

C   1 training period   2 training levy   3 on-the-job training, in-house training   4 tailor-made training

Presentations

A   1 slides   2 overhead projector   3 whiteboard/screen   4 podium/platform   5 marker pens   6 pointer   7 slide projector   8 microphone   9 flipcharts   10 lectern   11 carafe/bottle   12 ashtray

B   1 (guest) speakers, experts, personality, delegates, interpreters, organizer   2 papers, speeches, abstract, biography, programme, publicity material   3 abstract   4 eminent   5 theme   6 outlining   7 additional   8 simultaneous interpretation   9 speech   10 brief

C   1 ladies   2 gentlemen   3 pleasure   4 privilege   5 host   6 welcome   7 honour   8 open

Air Travel

A   1 ending   2 d   3 proceed   4 reclaim   5 indicating   6 clear   7 take   8 declare   9 transfer   10 follow   11 e   12 b   13 c   14 fare   15 a

B   1 departure lounge   2 gates   3 shopping mall   4 catering   5 duty   6 bureau   7 check-in   8 tagged   9 destination   10 monitors   11 baggage   12 customs

C   1 Germany   U.S.A.   U.S.S.R.   Australia   Netherlands   Israel   Greece   Spain   2 jumbo jet, boarding pass, long haul, flight number   3 take off   4 2.5 miles long   5 the red channel

Business-to-Business

A   1 businesses for sale   2 commercial property   3 leasing   4 equipment   5 business services   6   computers & computing services   7   translations   8 loans and finance   9 office supplies   10 legal services

B   1 a quarter of an inch   2 square feet   3 about £750,000   4 at   5 turnover   6 for/a   7 enquire, fax, send, ring   8 catalogue, leaflet, brochure, price list

C   1 accurate   2 record   3 automatically   4 contractual   5 profitable   6 territory   7 trading   8 growth   9 b   10 a

The Stock Market

A   1 listed securities, domestic, unlisted securities (USM), international   2 broker, fund manager, analyst, market maker   3 fixed-interest, equities   4 (fixed interest) loan, government and debenture stocks, preference shares (equities) deferred and ordinary

B   1 market maker   2 equities   3 broker   4 international   5 loan stocks   6 listed securities   7 fixed-interest   8 government stock   9 unlisted securities   10 analyst   11 domestic   12 fund manager   13 bear   14 bull   15 (a) share prices fall because there are more sellers than buyers (b) share prices rise because there are more buyers than sellers

C   1 blue-chip   2 investment   3 offer   4 unit trusts   5 bonds   6 portfolio   7 valuation   8 listing   9 flotation   10 trading   11 dividend   12 speculators

Contracts

A   1 act   2 participate   3 undertake   4 set up   5 be   6 provide   7 draw up   8 collect   9 produce   10 maintain   11 accept   12 authorize

B   1 C.I.I.   2 Not stated   3 C.P.C.O.   4 Not stated   5 C.I.I.   6 Not stated

C   1 hearing   2 consultant   3 arbitration   4 cancellation   5 clause   6 stipulation   7 terms   8 parties

Sponsorship

A 1 sponsoring   2 prime   3 boosted   4 capital
funding   5 supporting   6 prestigious   7 higher
profile   8 coverage   9 image   10 logo

B 1 b   2 c   3 e   4 a   5 f   6 d

C business expense, tax-deductible, multi-nationals,
mailing lists, target audience, insurance company

Terms of Employment

A 1 c   2 d   3 g   4 f   5 a   6 e   7 f   8 h

B 1 Dutch 2 Japanese 3 Japan 4 Sweden 5 U.S.

C 6 b   7 c   8 c   9 b   10 a

Patents

A 1 abstract   2 claims   3 drawings   4 submits
5 fees   6 filing date   7 documents
8 examination   9 publication   10 inspection
11 specification   12 grants

B 1 inventions   2 incentive   3 monopoly

4 exploitation   5 stimulate   6 technological
7 innovation   8 backlog   9 licensing
10 infringement   11 protection   12 litigation

C 1 Can an invention be exploited without a patent?
2 Does copyright only apply to the work of
authors?   3 Is a trademark always a design?
4 What does it mean when a patent is pending?

Business News

A 1 merger   2 joint venture   3 new appointment
4 market trends   5 labour dispute   6
environment-friendly products   7 job losses
8 legal action   9 + 3   10 + 4   11 + 2   12 + 6

B 1 location   2 chief   3 resigned   4 flat   5 sit-in
6 adjourned   7 know-how   8 top   9 trim
10 curb

C The watchdog Food Commission has said
chewing gum should carry a health warning on
the packet because it contains mineral
hydrocarbons banned from other foodstuffs.
Tobacco, cigarettes and cigars carry health
warnings in the U.K.

Franchising

A 1 food & drink   2 print   3 home improvements
4 transport (or business services)   5 convenience
retail   6 clothes & fashion   7 business &
professional services   8 vehicle maintenance &
repair   9 property-based   10 mobile/home
operators   11 mobile/home operators
12 business-to-business   13 business-to-business
14 retail sales

B 1 entrepreneurs   2 running   3 backgrounds
4 reputable   5 clearing   6 potential
7 franchisor   8 franchisee   9 screening
10 unsuitable

C 1 overheads, working capital, lease premium
2 tight controls, national advertising, company
back-up, ongoing training, quality specifications

Word List

This is a handy alphabetical list of 1,000 key business words and expressions featured in this book. You can use it both for reference, and as a framework for follow-up work. Up to three page references are provided for each item listed, so you can quickly find an example of its use(s) in context.

abstract 55, 68
accommodation 12, 36, 42
account 12, 16, 50
accountant 17, 49
accounts 12, 14
acquisition 58
actuary 7
add (up) 50
address (n) 17, 18, 26
address (v) 19, 49, 54
adjourn 70
adjuster 7
administration 12, 14, 26
administrator 12
admission 24
advance 15, 36, 62
advertise 13, 27, 32
advertisement 12, 33, 58
advertising 32, 33, 73
advice 41, 52, 63
advise 14
afford 69
agency 13, 33, 40
agenda 48, 49
agent 7, 18, 68
AGM (annual general meeting) 49
agree (to) 62
agreement 5, 62, 63
air waybill 4, 5
air-conditioned 42
airline 57
airport 40, 43, 56
allocate 37
allocation 65
allowance 39
amount 15, 30, 31
analysis 26, 52
analyst 60
annual 7, 45, 66
annual report 15
answer phone 8, 9
AOB (any other business) 48
apologies 48
appeal 33, 65
applicant 12, 68, 69
application 7, 12, 68
application form 17, 45
apply for 16, 68

appoint 12
appointment 1, 12, 66
appreciation 61
apprentice 53
arbitration 62
arrange 14, 63
arrangement 12, 59, 62
arrival 56
article 3, 27, 43
assessor 7
assets 15
association 64
attend 36, 39, 48
audio-visual 42, 43, 54
authorities 5
authority 9, 52, 61
authorize 9, 16, 63
automatic 28, 29, 59
availability 5, 47
available 7, 27, 50
average 3, 7, 67

backlog 69
back-up 51, 73
balance 52
ballot 49
ban 71, 73
bank 5, 30, 44
bank account 16, 17
bank sort code 17
banking 16, 45, 58
bar chart 3, 53, 67
bar code 21, 57
bargain 46
based (in) 12
bear 61
bear market 61
benefit 12, 13, 53
bid (n) 61
bid (v) 40
bill 16
bill of lading 4, 5
bit 11
black market 51
block booking 36
blue-chip 61
board meeting 49
board of directors 37

comprehensive 7, 34
computer 3, 10, 58
computing 11, 12, 58
conditions 34, 63, 66
confederation 62
conference 12, 36, 42
confirm 18, 31, 37
confirmation 5
congress 62
consortium 9
construction 27, 40
consultancy 41
consultant 12, 58, 62
consumer 20, 33, 46
consumer durables 46
contact (n) 12, 28, 41
contact (v) 17, 18, 45
contain 30, 57, 71
container 22, 23
containerization 22, 23
content 67, 52, 62
contents 21, 24, 28
contract 9, 62, 66
contractor 37, 70
contractual 59
contribution 66
convenient 18, 31, 35
conversion 50
convertible 60
co-ordination 12
copy 5, 18, 55
copyright 69, 70
copywriter 33
corporate 14, 36, 58
corporation 58
correspondence 14, 18, 19
cost (n) 6, 9, 34
cost (v) 9, 20, 45
cost-effective 41
costing 20, 52
costs 2, 23, 46
counter 45, 46
counterpart 67
coupon 32
course 14, 52, 53
court 70
cover (n) 7, 34
cover (v) 7, 34, 46
coverage 64
credit 31
credit card 16, 31, 51
creditor 16
crew 57
currency 45, 50, 51

current 34
current account 16, 17, 30
curriculum vitae 26, 27
customer 7, 14, 28
customs 5, 56, 57
customs declaration form 4, 5
cut 46, 70
cut-price 27, 72

data 3
data processing 14
database 11
day-release 39
deal (n) 71
deal (in) 60
deal (with) 7, 27
dealer 50
debenture stock 60
debit (n) 31
debit (v) 30
debt 15, 44, 63
decentralize 39
decision-making 15
declare 56, 57
decline 2
deferred share 60
delegate (n) 36, 43, 54
delegate (v) 39, 52
deliver 22
delivery 5, 14, 72
demand 2, 9, 21
demonstrator 32, 33
denomination 50, 51
department 12, 14, 15
department store 32, 47
departure 56, 57
deposit account 16, 17, 44
depot 47
deregulated 9
design 21, 29, 69
desk 57
destination 5, 57
details 17, 26, 58
development 12, 40, 49
dial 28, 29, 42
dictate 29
direct debit 17, 44
director 26, 65
directory 8
discharge 22
discount 7, 31, 36
discriminate 13
discrimination 27
discuss 28, 48, 49

discuss 37, 48, 49
disk drive 10, 11
display 3, 28, 46
dispute 12, 63, 70
distribute 58
distribution 20, 22, 47
distributor 58
dividend 27, 60, 61
dock 22
document 4, 28, 68
documentation 29, 56
dollar 51
domestic 56, 60
door-to-door 23, 72
dot matrix 11
double 43
draft 68
draw (up) 14, 48, 63
drawing 68
driving licence 34
duties 13
duty - free 57

earnings 3
EC (European Community) 9
economical 23
economy 15, 60
electronic 5, 30, 47
employ 7, 14
employee 14, 41, 66
employer 6, 27, 66
employment 13, 36, 66
employment agency 72
enclosure 18
endorsement 34
engaged 9, 29
engineer 26
enterprise 27, 52
entitled 66, 67
entitlement 66, 67
entrepreneur 27, 73
envelope 19, 58
equipment 5, 11, 64
equity 60
establish 58, 73
estimate 34, 48, 52
European Community 53
exchange (n) 45, 51
exchange (v) 45, 50, 51
excluding 3
exclusive 42, 43, 59
executive 12, 27, 43
executor 44
exhibition 42

expand 11, 12, 27
expansion 11
expenditure 52, 59, 62
expense 65
expense account 39
expenses 6, 38, 50
expensive 9, 44, 56
experience 5, 12, 27
experienced 12, 27
expert 55, 63
expertise 12
expire 30
exploitation 69
export 4, 12, 41
exporter 5
extend 12
extension 9, 26

f.a.s. (free alongside ship) 5
f.o.b. (free on board) 5
facilities 39, 42, 44
factory 14
faithfully 75
fall (n) 61
fall (v) 2
fare 27, 56
fall 5, 28, 40
feature (n) 28
feature (v) 41
fee 36, 62, 68
figure 9, 65
figures 3, 52, 70
file 68
fill (in) 5, 35, 68
finance (n) 41, 58, 73
finance (v) 60
financial 12, 17, 41
firm 14, 39, 40
fixed-interest 60
flat 70
fleet 34, 35, 42
flexitime 39, 66, 67
flight 56, 57
floppy disk 11
dlotation 61
flowchart 68
fluctuate 2, 45
fluctuation 61
for sale 20, 58, 61
forecast 50
forecasting 52
foreign currency 44, 45, 50
foreign exchange 50
form 5, 16, 68

forward 25
forward (v) 34
franchise 40, 73
franchisee 73
franchising 72, 73
franchisor 72, 73
free 32, 39, 58
freight 5, 23, 27
fringe benefit 38, 39
fuel 23
full-time 43
function 14, 15, 33
fund (v) 53
fund manager 60
funding 64
funds 61

gate 56, 57
GDP (gross domestic product) 53
gilt-edged 61
gimmick 32, 33
giro 16
goods 5, 14, 47
government stock 60
grade 22
graduate 12
grant 68
graph 2, 3
graphics 3, 11, 21
group 9
grow 3, 43
growth 9, 15, 58
guarantee (n) 5, 30, 46
guarantee (v) 7, 45, 73
guideline 37

handle 7, 12, 56
hands on 27
handset 8
hard disk 11
hardware 10, 58
haulage 23
head office 42
headhunter 13
headline 58
headquarters 1, 14
hearing 62
high-level 11
high-resolution 11
hire (n) 34, 35, 42
hire (v) 34, 35
hold (n) 22
hold (v) 30, 48, 62
hold (on) 10

holding 61
hours 34, 39, 66
hypermarket 47

illegal 13, 51
image 33, 64, 65
import 4, 5, 40
importer 58
in charge of 14, 44
in lieu 66
incentive 39, 69
include 7, 11, 34
inclusive 42
income 3, 7, 61
incoming 14, 19
increase 2, 3, 46
increment 66
indemnity 36
industrial 12, 61, 72
industry 62
inflation 3
information 2, 15, 24
infringement 69
in-house 15, 53, 65
innovation 69
inquiry 43
in-store 33
instructions 21, 29, 56
insurance 5, 6, 34
insure 5
intellectual property rights 69
interest 3, 44, 60
interest-free 38, 45
internal 14, 15
international 9, 12, 60
interpreter 55
interpreting 58
interview 66
invention 68, 69
inventor 69
invest 61
investment 60, 61
investor 60, 61
invoice 24, 35
irrevocable 5
issue 5, 45, 60
item 10, 20, 48
itinerary 18

job 7, 12, 53
joint venture 41, 58, 70
junior 39
junk mail 25

senior 12, 43, 66
service (n) 9, 19, 35
service (v) 72
services 7, 14, 59
session 36, 37
set up 40, 52, 63
setting 28
settle 7
settling 63
share 9, 15, 60
shareholder 49
shelf life 46
shift 39
ship (v) 5
shipment 5
shopping mall 57
sign 17, 19, 63
signature 18
sincerely 18, 19
single 10, 40, 43
sir 19
site 40, 47, 71
skill 12, 26, 52
slogan 33
small business 40, 69
software 11, 58
sole trader 15
solicitor 58
source 58
space 37, 58
speaker 12, 37, 54
specialist 12, 14, 70
specialist (n) 61, 62
specialize 12, 27, 61
specification 11, 68, 73
speculator 61
speech 36, 37, 55
spend (n) 33
spend (v) 30, 45, 50
sponsor (n) 64
sponsor (v) 64, 65
sponsorship 64, 65
spreadsheet 3, 11
staff 7, 15, 38
stamp 19
standard 14, 41
standard shipping note 4
standing order 16, 17, 44
statement 17, 24
statistics 2, 3, 26
status 49, 61, 64
statutory 66
sterling 45
stipulate 34

stipulation 62
stock (n) 5, 32, 60
stock (v) 47
stock exchange 15, 60, 61
stock market 60, 61
store (n) 46, 47, 72
store (v) 17, 21
strategy 20
streamline 22
structure 14
submit 49, 68
subscribe 15
subscriber 9, 61
subscription 24, 61
subsidiary 12
subsidize 38
subm 16, 27
supplement 39
supplier 12, 40, 72
supplies 14, 58
supply 70
support (n) 12
support (v) 64
survey 43
switchboard 8, 9
system 5, 11, 35

tailor-made 43, 53
take off 57
take over 27
target 25, 33
target audience 65
tariff 43
tax 3, 59
tax-deductible 65
team 12, 22, 52
teamwork 39
technical 11, 12, 68
technological 69
telecommunications 9
telephone 9, 30, 34
telephoning 8
telex 29
temporary 69
terminal 30, 56, 57
terms 34, 62, 66
territory 59
test marketing 40
third party 34
total 67, 70
track record 13
trade 5, 47, 72
trade fair 41
trade union 49, 66